Self-Esteem

Activities to Build Self-Worth

Grades 2-3

Published by World Teachers Press®
www.worldteacherspress.com

Published with the permission of R.I.C. Publications Pty. Ltd.

Copyright © 2007 by Didax, Inc., Rowley, MA 01969. All rights reserved.

First published by R.I.C. Publications Pty. Ltd., Perth, Western Australia. Revised by Didax Educational Resources.

Printed in the United States of America.

Order Number: 2-5271
ISBN-13: 978-1-58324-252-0

A B C D E F 11 10 09 08 07

395 Main Street
Rowley, MA 01969
www.didax.com

Foreword

Addressing self-esteem and social resilience in students is fundamental to creating a safe, happy learning environment. *Self-Esteem, Grades 2 to 3* is a resource for investigating personal and social issues faced by elementary school-aged students. The activity topics in this book have been carefully selected to address issues specific to lower elementary-aged students with a view to building self-worth and establishing resilience in challenging situations. All activities are suitable for whole-class instruction or for use with individuals or small groups with particular needs. Other titles in this series are:

Self-Esteem, Grades 4 to 5
Self-Esteem, Grades 6 to 8

Contents

All students will encounter challenges, personally and socially, at school. *Self-Esteem, Grades 2 to 3* looks at a comprehensive range of these issues to equip students with positive beliefs about themselves and a resilient attitude. By using the activities in this book, students will be encouraged to value and implement practices that promote personal growth and well-being. Students who are self-motivated and confident in their approach to life will extend this philosophy to learning, enabling them to work successfully in individual and collaborative situations, while recognizing that everyone has the right to feel valued and be safe. Students will be encouraged to understand their rights as a student and community member and, in turn, their obligations and the requirement to behave responsibly.

Issues addressed within this series include: self-management skills, interpersonal skills, attitudes and values, decision-making, goal-setting, interpersonal communication, cooperation, collaboration, relationship-building, group dynamics, child protection, bullying and harassment, and concepts for developing a healthy, happy lifestyle.

Teacher Notes

Each activity is accompanied by detailed teacher notes to assist teachers in planning, implementing and monitoring the concepts addressed.

Concept

Explains the concept being addressed

Indicators

Indicators for students' progress are included to provide teachers with clear concepts for teaching and monitoring. These indicators can also be incorporated into student assessment pieces.

Using the Student Activity Sheet

Detailed step-by-step instructions are included to assist teachers in prompting student understanding and guiding discussion appropriately.

Follow-Up Suggestions

Additional activities will help students internalize new skills or understandings by reviewing them or applying them to real-life and lifelike situations.

Pre-Lesson Focus Discussion

Questions, discussion topics and, in some cases, introductory activities have been provided to focus students on the topic prior to completing the more formal written tasks on the student activity sheet.

Sensitivity Issues

Many of the topics cannot be addressed in a way which meets the needs of all students equally. The information in this section is to remind teachers of the varying needs of the individuals in their care and to be mindful of sensitive situations which may exist.

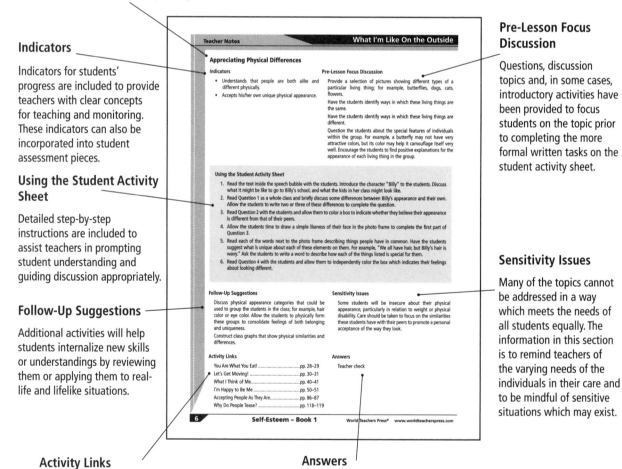

Activity Links

A list of related activities accompanies each task and may be used as follow-up learning activities.

Answers

Answers have been provided where necessary. However, in most activities, answers are based on student experiences and self-assessment and should not be assessed formally. Informal monitoring by teachers is a more appropriate means of gathering information about students so as to guide and assist them in their personal and social growth.

Student Activity Sheet

Each student activity sheet is written at a level suitable for grades two to three, incorporating written tasks and age-appropriate activities.

Cartoon

Each activity is supported by a focusing cartoon designed to capture the students' imagination and provoke discussion about the topic or issue to be investigated.

Opportunities for Reflection

Students are encouraged to reflect upon their own life and existing beliefs within the context of new concepts. In many cases, they will be asked to assess the effectiveness or appropriateness of their own behavior.

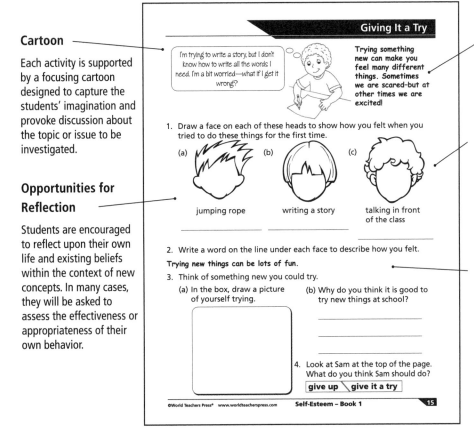

Discussion Text

A short discussion text briefly outlines the concept being investigated and provides direction for the tasks within the activity sheet.

Opportunities for Clarification

In most activities, students will be prompted to clarify new concepts being taught through relating them to their own life and experiences.

Opportunities for Application

Students are encouraged to internalize new information and apply it to their existing belief system, often challenging them to address existing behavior in order to develop themselves personally and socially.

Assessment

Many of the activities within the series can be used to indicate social skills development in student portfolios. Note: Activities where students have disclosed sensitive information are not appropriate for assessment.

Appreciating Physical Differences

Indicators

- Understands that people are both alike and different physically.
- Accepts his/her own unique physical appearance.

Pre-Lesson Focus Discussion

Provide a selection of pictures showing different types of a particular living thing; for example, butterflies, dogs, cats, flowers.

Have the students identify ways in which these living things are the same.

Have the students identify ways in which these living things are different.

Question the students about the special features of individuals within the group. For example, a butterfly may not have very attractive colors, but its color may help it camouflage itself very well. Encourage the students to find positive explanations for the appearance of each living thing in the group.

Using the Student Activity Sheet

1. Read the text inside the speech bubble with the students. Introduce the character "Billy" to the students. Discuss what it might be like to go to Billy's school, and what the kids in her class might look like.
2. Read Question 1 as a whole class and briefly discuss some differences between Billy's appearance and their own. Allow the students to write two or three of these differences to complete the question.
3. Read Question 2 with the students and allow them to color a box to indicate whether they believe their appearance is different from that of their peers.
4. Allow the students time to draw a simple likeness of their face in the photo frame to complete the first part of Question 3.
5. Read each of the words next to the photo frame describing things people have in common. Have the students suggest what is unique about each of these elements on them. For example, "We all have hair, but Billy's hair is wavy." Ask the students to write a word to describe how each of the things listed is special for them.
6. Read Question 4 with the students and allow them to independently color the box which indicates their feelings about looking different.

Follow-Up Suggestions

Discuss physical appearance categories that could be used to group the students in the class; for example, hair color or eye color. Allow the students to physically form these groups to consolidate feelings of both belonging and uniqueness.

Construct class graphs that show physical similarities and differences.

Sensitivity Issues

Some students will be insecure about their physical appearance, particularly in relation to weight or physical disability. Care should be taken to focus on the similarities these students have with their peers to promote a personal acceptance of the way they look.

Activity Links

Answers

Teacher check

Hi! I'm Billy. There are lots of kids in my class. But I don't look like the other kids. Even though we are all kids, we all look different.

1. Write some ways Billy looks different from you.

_____

_____

_____

2. Do you look exactly the same as the other students in your class?

Yes \ No

3. Draw a portrait of yourself. Write a word to describe each of these things.

    (a) hair _____

    (b) skin _____

    (c) eyes _____

    (d) nose _____

    (e) face _____

4. Do you like looking different from the other people in your class?

Yes \ No

Recognizing Personal Qualities

Indicators

- Understands there are things about people which can be seen, such as appearance and behavior.
- Understands people have personal qualities that cannot be seen but can be expressed.
- Aspires to internalize personal qualities that generate a positive sense of self.

Pre-Lesson Focus Discussion

Brainstorm to list "good" and "not-so-good" qualities of people. Prompt the students with suggestions such as "kind," "sharing," or "mean." The students may use slang to describe some qualities. This slang need not be discouraged as it can assist the students in understanding some of the subtle traits they do not yet know the words to describe. Offer a more suitable word if appropriate.

Sort a selection of personal and physical qualities into "outside" things (those that can be physically seen by others) and "inside" things (those we can express or feel).

Using the Student Activity Sheet

1. Read the text in Billy's speech bubble with the students. Ask them to clarify what they think Billy means by what she is like on the "inside."
2. Read the first sentence on the activity sheet and ask the students to take turns reading the qualities listed in the flower petals. Encourage the students to suggest other personal qualities that have not been included in the flower. Students can add extra petals if they would like to write further personal qualities.
3. Read Question 1 as a class. Identify those qualities which could be classified as "good" and those which are "not-so-good." Allow the students time to think about each quality honestly and color it if they think it is a quality they have inside them.
4. Discuss which qualities are most desirable and why. Accept different opinions, as students will see different qualities as important based upon their experiences and their personal strengths. Read Question 2 (a) as a class and have the students write their three most important traits in the boxes provided. They can use words on the petals or their own.
5. Read 2 (b) together and encourage the students to suggest ways in which the selected qualities could be demonstrated. Have the students write a simple sentence for each of the qualities listed.

Follow-Up Suggestions

Play a game of charades where the students have to act out a good deed; for example, giving someone half of his/her morning snack or allowing someone to play. Discuss the personal qualities demonstrated through these gestures.

Keep a supply of "good deed" awards for students who demonstrate commendable personal qualities by way of a good deed. Ask the student's peers to suggest the positive personal qualities that should be listed on the award.

Sensitivity Issues

Identifying positive personal qualities is a great way for teachers to consolidate the good behavior of students in their class. All students love praise, though some may find receiving praise awkward. Remember to give praise carefully and genuinely. Make a conscious effort to separate bad behavior from personal qualities, and use these opportunities to demonstrate that what we do and how we look on the outside do not necessarily describe a person on the inside. Give students opportunities to demonstrate their positive traits through good deeds, and be on the lookout for opportunities to give immediate positive feedback.

Activity links

Answers

Teacher check

> Everyone can see what I am like on the outside—but I think what I'm like on the inside is what makes me really special!

Here are some qualities we can have on the inside. Can you think of any others?

1. Think about the word in each petal of the flower. Color the petal if you think the word describes what you are like.

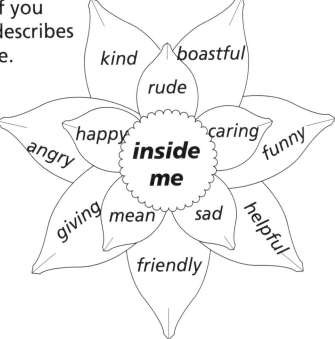

2. (a) Write a word in each of the boxes below that describes what you most want to be like.

   (b) Next to each word, write a way you could show others you have this quality inside you.

Recognizing Skills And Talents

Indicators

- Identifies personal skills and talents.
- Appreciates his/her skills and talents.
- Understands that people can be "specialists" or "all-rounders."

Pre-Lesson Focus Discussion

Encourage the students to "show and tell" something they are particularly good at or that is unique to them; for example, singing a song, sharing a collection, or showing an award.

Discuss why some people are good at some things and some are good at others.

Talk about how it makes them feel to be particularly good at something.

Interview the students who have identified their special "thing" to find out how it became special for them.

Using the Student Activity Sheet

1. Read the text in the speech bubble with the students. Discuss what makes Sam believe he is good at spelling and how he became good at it.

2. Encourage the students to share with their peers the things they are good at. Construct a list of "Things We Are Good At" and keep it on display for the students. Have selected students demonstrate their skills and talents if they would like to.

3. Read Question 1 with the students and have them write on the ladder examples of things they are good at. Ensure the list constructed earlier by the class is available for them to view and assist them in completing the task.

4. Ask the students whether they have one very special thing they are good at or if they are good at many things. Allow them to mark "one" or "many" to complete Question 2. Explain that often children do not find out what they are very good at until they are much older, and many people become good at lots of things rather than becoming very good at one thing.

5. Read Question 3 as a class and allow the students time to draw a picture of themselves doing something that is or could be special for them.

Follow-Up Suggestions

Have "specialists" in different fields come to the class to speak with the students about their "special" thing and how they became very good at it; for example, singers, artists, computer technicians, athletes, medical people.

Encourage the students to develop a step-by-step chart to help them become a "specialist" at something, using the activity sheet on page 11.

Sensitivity Issues

Many students may be discouraged if they have not identified a special skill or talent yet. Ensure the students understand that we need to try many things before we can determine what we really like doing or are really good at. Introduce the concept of being an "all-rounder"—someone who is not a "specialist" at anything but is good at many different kinds of things. This will encourage students to keep trying and appreciating new things. Being an "all-rounder" should be valued equally with being a "specialist."

Activity Links

Answers

Teacher check

I'm Sam. I won this ribbon at a spelling bee. I really enjoy spelling and practice hard to get better by studying words.

We can be good at lots of things.

1. Think of some things you are good at. Write them on the ladder.

Some people have one special thing they are very good at. Others have many things they can do.

2. Are you very good at one thing or good at many things?

    | **One** | **Many** |

3. Draw yourself doing your special thing in the space below. If you don't have a special thing, draw yourself doing something you would like to be very good at one day.

Being Responsible

Indicators

- Understands that everyone is responsible for certain jobs, including them.
- Identifies his/her own responsibilities.

Pre-Lesson Focus Discussion

Discuss what a job is. Have the students relate jobs that their parents do and why they need to do the jobs. Talk about what might happen if adults did not do their jobs. Where would we go if we were sick? Would there be any schools? Where would we get food to eat?

Encourage the students to share their ideas on why doing a job is important. Introduce the concept of being responsible and how it would feel to be responsible for a special job.

Allow the students to share jobs they are responsible for at home and what would happen if they were not responsible and did not do them.

Using the Student Activity Sheet

1. Look at the drawing with the students. Discuss the job it illustrates.
2. Read the text in bold print at the top of the page with the students and have them answer the question "What are your jobs at home?" verbally. Encourage them to share their jobs with the class.
3. Read the school jobs on the "notice board" in Question 1. Ask the students to color the jobs on the notice board they have to do or have had to do in the past.
4. Discuss which jobs need to be done by everyone every day and which only need to be done sometimes. Have the students select three jobs they have to do every day and write them in the spaces provided to complete Question 2.
5. Refer the students back to the discussion held earlier about jobs they have to do at home before they complete Question 3.

Follow-Up Suggestions

Make a class chart of jobs to be done. Nominate different students to be "monitors" for the jobs every day.

Have a designated time during the day for doing "special" jobs to help the students remember. Praise the students for remembering special jobs without being reminded.

Make a checklist of responsible class behavior and keep it displayed for the students to refer to. Include things such as "I tidy the floor," "I am a good listener," "I finish my work."

Sensitivity Issues

Students love to be given responsibility. Those who feel they can be trusted to do important jobs become confident and responsible. If some students are given preference, sensitive students who are left out may develop a sense of being mistrusted or irresponsible. Be careful to give equal opportunities to students who are known to be reliable as to those who need to work on becoming reliable. Team students in pairs so they can be accountable to one another.

Activity Links

Playing Safe ....pp. 38–39

Friends Chain ....pp. 76–77

Be Careful! ....pp. 78–79

Doing Your Best...............................pp. 82–83

Answers

Teacher check

Everyone has jobs to do. What are your jobs at home? We have jobs to do at school as well.

1. Read the jobs on the notice board. Color the jobs you have done at school.

cleaned the board	put away the play equipment	put trash in the trashcan	carried my school bag
wrote in my diary	passed out books	put my lunch box away	tidied up the floor
fed the class pet	sharpened pencils	watered the class plants	

Some jobs have to be done every day. Some jobs we only have to do sometimes.

2. Write two jobs you have to do at school every day.

3. (a) Draw a picture of yourself doing one of your jobs at home.

   (b) What is the job?

   _____

   (c) Who do you help by doing this job?

Sensible Risk-Taking

Indicators

- Demonstrates a willingness to try new things.
- Understands that sometimes trying new things requires risk-taking.
- Understands people can learn from making mistakes.

Pre-Lesson Focus Discussion

Describe or draw an elaborate rollercoaster ride for the students. Ask them if they would like to ride on it. Encourage them to share how they would feel before riding on the rollercoaster ride. How would they decide whether they should go on it or not? Is it a risk? Could anything go wrong? What would be a good decision?

Have the students form a line, one behind the other, and walk into a circle so that the line is continuous. Ask the students to crouch down in the line with their hands on the shoulders of the person in front of them. Describe the ride again and have the students "follow the leader" to act out the ups, downs and sideways movements as the ride progresses.

When finished, ask the students if they enjoyed the ride. Are they glad they took the risk?

Using the Student Activity Sheet

1. Read the text in the thought bubble with the students. Ask the students whether they have ever been in a situation similar to Sam's. Encourage them to share their situation and how they felt.
2. Read the text in bold type at the top of the page. Refer to the rollercoaster experience to demonstrate the different emotions people can experience when trying something new.
3. Direct the students to Question 1. Read the subheading under each of the heads and allow the students to draw a face to describe how they felt about trying each of the activities.
4. To complete Question 2, have the students write a word describing each of the emotions they drew.
5. Brainstorm to list some new things with the class that they could "give a try." Ask the students to choose something from the list or something different of their own as a focus for completing Question 3. Encourage the students to share their thoughts on why "giving it a try" is a good thing.
6. Refer to Sam's predicament at the top of the page. Read Question 4 with the students and allow them to mark it appropriately.

Follow-Up Suggestions

Give awards to students for "giving it a try" to encourage sensible risk-taking.

Develop a collage of "new things" the class has experienced to display on the classroom wall. Add text to the display such as "brave," "exciting," "scary," "fun" and "We gave it a try!"

Sensitivity Issues

Where some students will be willing to try anything, others may be very cautious, depending on their personality. To a large extent, these traits may be innate. Therefore, the goal is not to alter the students' natural response to a challenging situation but to equip them with skills to help them make good decisions and take sensible risks. By creating a classroom environment that is warm, consistent and respectful, students will gain the security they need to take risks in their learning and learn from mistakes.

Activity Links

Answers

Teacher check

I'm trying to write a story, but I don't know how to write all the words I need. I'm a bit worried—what if I get it wrong?

Trying something new can make you feel many different things. Sometimes we are scared–but at other times we are excited!

1. Draw a face on each of these heads to show how you felt when you tried to do these things for the first time.

(a)

jumping rope

(b)

writing a story

(c)

talking in front of the class

2. Write a word on the line under each face to describe how you felt.

Trying new things can be lots of fun.

3. Think of something new you could try.

(a) In the box, draw a picture of yourself trying.

(b) Why do you think it is good to try new things at school?

_____

_____

_____

4. Look at Sam at the top of the page. What do you think Sam should do?

| give up | give it a try |

Learning From Mistakes

Indicators

- Understands people can learn from making mistakes.
- Understands that making mistakes when learning something new is not foolish.
- Demonstrates a willingness to show sensitivity to others when they make mistakes.

Pre-Lesson Focus Discussion

Role-play mistakes the students might make in situations inside or outside the classroom. Discuss whether it was worth taking the risk of making a mistake in each of those situations.

Encourage the students to share situations where they have been worried about making a mistake.

Using the Student Activity Sheet

1. Look at the cartoon at the top of the student activity sheet. Ask the students whether something similar has ever happened to them. How did they feel? Did anyone say anything? Do anything? Did they want to try again or give up?

2. Read together the text in bold print at the top of the page. Ask the students whether they think Billy's classmates will think she is silly. Have them mark "yes" or "no" and write a justification to complete Question 1.

3. Ask the students about the mistakes they have made. Stress that mistakes do not need to be bad things and that most people make them when they learn something new. Share a mistake you have made with the students or "accidentally" make a spelling mistake as you write something on the board.

4. Direct the students to the picture in Question 2. Discuss what is happening in the picture and have the students brainstorm to list some mistakes the boy risks making by learning to play the game. Allow the students time to use the information from this discussion to complete Questions 2 (a) and (b).

5. Read each of the words in the boxes in Question 2 (c). Have the students color the boxes containing the response or responses they would make to the boy's mistakes. Discuss the merits of, or problems with, each.

Follow-Up Suggestions

Role-play appropriate and inappropriate responses to mistakes other people make. Discuss the impact each response would have on the person who made the mistake.

Construct a class big book titled "We All Make Mistakes." Have the students draw pictures of their mistake and complete the sentence "I learned ..." underneath each. Read the book to the class and make it available to the students during quiet reading times.

Sensitivity Issues

Fear of disapproval by peers can be a powerful emotion and requires considerable bravery and resolve to overcome. It is important to first give opportunities for less adventurous students to take risks in controlled situations where they will not be scrutinized by their peers. While encouraging the students to engage in challenging tasks is the goal, emphasis and praise must also be dedicated to the appropriate responses, and encouragement given by peers.

Activity Links

Answers

Teacher check

Sometimes we can be worried about making mistakes or looking silly. But making a mistake can be a great way to learn the things we are not sure about. Billy learned a word she didn't know by "giving it a try" and trying hard.

1. Do you think everyone will think she is a Silly Billy? | Yes | No |
   Why?

_____

Have you ever made a mistake? People make mistakes while they are learning to do all kinds of new things—even adults!

2. This boy is learning to play soccer.

   (a) Write a mistake he might make learning soccer.

   _____

   _____

   (b) Write what you think he will learn from making this mistake.

   _____

   _____

   _____

   (c) Color what you would do if you saw someone make a mistake like his.

   | laugh | help | tease |

   | smile kindly | say nothing |

Trying Hard

Indicators

- Understands that making mistakes is part of learning.
- Understands that some things take a long time to complete.
- Appreciates the satisfaction gained from completing difficult or time-consuming tasks properly.

Pre-Lesson Focus Discussion

Bring an example of something that took you a long time or was difficult to complete; for example, a complicated jigsaw puzzle or a tapestry. Take time to marvel at the detail and the involved process required to complete the task. Tell the students how long it took to do and encourage them to suggest how they think you may have felt when you started, during the process and when you completed the task.

Have the students share experiences they may have had completing a task. Focus questioning on how they felt before, during and after completing their task.

Using the Student Activity Sheet

1. Look at the cartoon at the top of the student page. Discuss what is happening in the picture.

2. Encourage the students to share things they made lots of mistakes in before learning to do them well.

3. Read Question 1 as a class. Talk about the things we say in our heads that we don't verbalize. Give the students time to explore the difference by saying something to themselves in their mind and then telling something to a friend. Have the students imagine they are doing something very difficult. To complete Question 1, allow them time to write what they would say to themselves while doing this task.

4. Direct the students to the three people in the pictures in Question 2. Read what each person is saying. To complete Question 2, ask the students to color the person they think would be the best learner and then circle the person most like themselves.

5. Discuss things that take a long time to finish. The students may wish to share specific tasks they have completed. Allow the students to complete Question 3 to describe a personal experience they have had with a task that took them a long time to complete.

Follow-Up Suggestions

Make a large outline of a shape relating to class work currently being studied. For example, draw a large character from the class reading book for the week or from a song being taught. Cut up colored paper into one-inch squares and have the students use them to make a collage on designated color areas to create a colorful mosaic picture. Discuss the emotions the students are feeling as they begin, during the process and when they finish this time-consuming task. Title the mosaic "Try Hard, Keep Going and Get the Job Done!"

Sensitivity Issues

Students facing difficult tasks often need more than encouragement to keep going. They will also need a plan of attack and a series of smaller, attainable goals to achieve during the process. Assist the students to plan and set goals as they embark on challenging tasks. Allow them to break a task into small, regular chunks. This will be more rewarding than persevering with an exhausted attitude.

Activity Links

Answers

Teacher check

 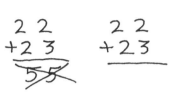

Some things can be hard work to learn. We sometimes make lots of mistakes before we can do them well.

1. What do you say to yourself when something is hard to learn?

_____

_____

2. Look at these three children. What are they saying to themselves?

(a) Color the person you think would be best at learning.

(b) Put a circle around the person who is most like you.

This is too hard for me. I can't do it.

This is hard work but I know if I keep trying I can do it.

This is hard work. I'll just do the parts I already know. That will do.

Some things can take a long time to finish. We have to try hard to keep going and get the job done.

3. (a) Write something that took you a long time to do.

_____

_____

(b) How long did it take?

about an hour	about a day
about a week	more than a week

(c) What did you say to yourself while you were doing it?

_____

_____

(d) Color how you felt when you were finished.

tired	pleased	proud
sad	glad to be finished	

Celebrating Achievements

Indicators

- Recognizes personal achievements.
- Feels pride in own achievements.
- Celebrates own achievements.

Pre-Lesson Focus Discussion

Bring in a special award for the students to view, such as a certificate, trophy, or medal. Encourage the students to bring in special awards they or other family members may have received. Discuss the types of achievements that medals and trophies can be awarded for.

Brainstorm to list other types of achievements. Discuss why some of the things we achieve are worth celebrating. Encourage the students to share something special they would like to achieve one day.

Using the Student Activity Sheet

1. Provide the students with the certificate on page 21. Read through the achievement award together and work out what needs to go in each blank space.

2. With the assistance of teachers, class helpers and peers, decide upon a special award for each student. Write each individual's achievement onto his/her award in front of the class.

3. While the awards are being written, have the students make a collage in the rectangle below "Let's Celebrate!" with festive materials such as glitter, confetti, stickers and streamers.

4. Present the awards at a special class achievement presentation party.

Follow-Up Suggestions

Invite a guest speaker with a special award such as a service medal or a sports medal. Have him/her tell his/her story of achievement and how it was celebrated.

Hold an "achievement celebration" party with the class where every class member is given a special award for something achieved at school.

Sensitivity Issues

While inclusiveness is important, achievements need to be earned to be significant to the students. Be careful to only present students with awards that are consistent with their efforts or behavior—rather than effort or behavior that is inconsistent. Achievement awards are valuable for recognizing mastery and effort, and for consolidating a student's image of himself/herself.

Activity Links

Answers

Teacher check

VERY SPECIAL ACHIEVEMENT

Awarded to

_____

for

_____

Let's Celebrate!

Teacher's signature   Date

_____

Setting Achievable Short-Term Goals

Indicators

- Determines a path of smaller, achievable steps to achieve a goal.
- Understands that setting short-term goals will assist him/her in achieving longer-term goals.
- Experiences satisfaction in achieving a goal through a series of small steps.

Pre-Lesson Focus Discussion

Set the students the task of making an extra-long paper chain—perhaps one that stretches across the classroom. Ask the students how long they think it would take. Ask them to suggest ways the chain could be made. Which is most efficient? Which seems the easiest? Provide the students with strips of colored paper and make a class plan for everyone to make a short section of the chain. When finished, each can add his/her small part to the chain to create the required length.

Reflect upon the effort required when the task was broken into small parts. Also consider the importance of having a plan before starting and how that helped them to know exactly what to do and how to do it. Use the chain to illustrate how many small parts combine to achieve a larger goal.

Using the Student Activity Sheet

1. Look at the cartoon and read the text in bold print at the top of the student activity page with the students. Discuss examples of tasks that seem as though they would take too long or would be too hard to do.

2. Use one of the students' examples to demonstrate how it could be broken down into small parts. Prepare an enlarged version of the footprints on the student activity sheet already cut out.

3. Glue the enlarged footprints to make a path up a long strip of colored paper for the students to view. Decide which of the students' examples will be used as a focus and determine what the goal is.

4. Have the students suggest how the task could be broken into smaller tasks to make it easier. Discuss each suggestion and how it could work to help achieve the goal. Write an appropriate short-term goal onto the first foot, and tell the students that they should wait to see how they do with that one before they decide the next goal. Discuss why they might need to wait and see before adding more.

5. Read the instructions on the activity sheet with the students. Allow them to cut out the footprints and glue them onto a colored paper strip of their own. Allow room for students to glue more footprints if required. Encourage the students to share their goals and determine what a good short-term stepping stone might be. When each student has established a reasonable short-term goal, allow him/her to write it in the first footprint.

6. Review the footprint strip the following day. Have the students determine whether or not they reached their short-term goal and color their footprint if they did. Students who have not can spend another day working on their first footprint or alter their goal so that it can be easily achieved the next day. Those who do achieve their goal can write another for the following day on the next footprint.

7. When all of the footprints have been completed, direct the students back to the beginning of their footprints and reread the goals they have achieved. Discuss how setting short-term goals helped to achieve a bigger, long-term goal.

Follow-Up Suggestions

Encourage students to practice goal-setting by completing homework tasks in day-by-day increments.

Establish "star charts" to plot increments of improvement; for example, books read or demonstration of improving behavior.

Activity Links

Sensitivity Issues

For students to experience success in goal-setting, each short-term goal must be seen as achievable by them. Encourage the students to be realistic in their goal-setting. Model goal-setting daily by using step-by-step instructions to complete class activities. While many people are capable of following up to five verbal instructions at a time, no more than two or three should be given at a time to young students in a classroom setting, and these should be repeated.

I want to build a playhouse ... but it's going to take forever! Where do I start?

Some things seem too hard to do. Some things seem like they will take too long. Why not try setting yourself an easy goal every day? When you do a little bit every day, big jobs don't look so hard after all!

1. Cut out the footprints below.

2. Glue the footprints on a long strip of colored paper.

3. Write an easy goal for tomorrow in the first footprint.

4. When you reach your goal, color in the footprint and write another easy goal in the next footprint for the following day.

When all of the footprints have been colored, look back at all the things you have done and see what you have achieved!!

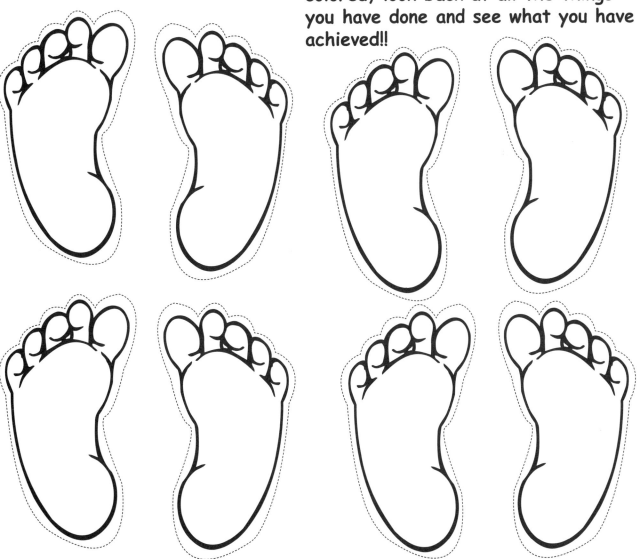

Encouraging a Positive Self-image

Indicators

- Acknowledges the good things about himself/herself.
- Acknowledges what makes him or her likable.
- Suggests ways to use his or her good points to be happy and successful.

Pre-Lesson Focus Discussion

Role-play for the students a person who is boastful. For example, you might boast about a great looking shirt you are wearing and suggest it is better than theirs. Encourage the students to talk about why the way you were talking was not appropriate. Discuss why people might not like boasters or "show-offs."

Explain there are ways to be confident and like yourself without boasting. It is okay to talk about your good points sometimes, as long as you don't hurt other people by making them feel less important. Have the students form a circle and say something nice about themselves without boasting or hurting the feelings of others.

Using the Student Activity Sheet

1. Read the text in the speech bubble with the students. Ask them to share something special about a classmate. You may be able to encourage the students by paying a compliment to another staff member who visits the room.

2. Direct the students to Question 1 and allow them to color "yes" or "no" independently to describe how they feel about themselves.

3. Read the text in bold that follows with the students. Hold a "silent minute" while the students close their eyes and think about what their good points are and how they could make the most of them to be a happy, successful person.

4. Describe how to complete the figurine cutout by reading the directions in Question 2. Allow the students time to cut, fold, color and write to complete the task.

5. Have the students share one of their good points with the class and suggest how they hope to make the most of it in the future.

Follow-Up Suggestions

Use suggestions the students may make about their good points as goals to work toward, using the footprint activity on page 23.

Introduce the importance of listening to others and how this makes people feel as though they are valued. Stress the importance of listening in activities where the students share their strengths.

Sensitivity Issues

Students who do not wish to share information about themselves can be encouraged, but not forced to participate. Talking about oneself is inappropriate in some cultures.

Discourage the students from using examples of show-offs in class discussions. Guide the discussion so the focus is on behaviors rather than individuals who demonstrate them.

Activity Links

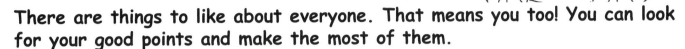

The way I look, the way I behave and the way I feel inside make me different from everyone else—and they make me a very special kid. I love being me!

1. Do you like being you? **Yes** **No**

There are things to like about everyone. That means you too! You can look for your good points and make the most of them.

2. (a) Draw your face on the figure below. Write your name in the box and draw and color in some clothes to make it look like you.

   (b) Cut along lines A and B.

(c) Fold along the fold line and then cut around the figure along the dotted line to create a "fold-out" person.

(d) Write some of your good points inside the folded sheet.

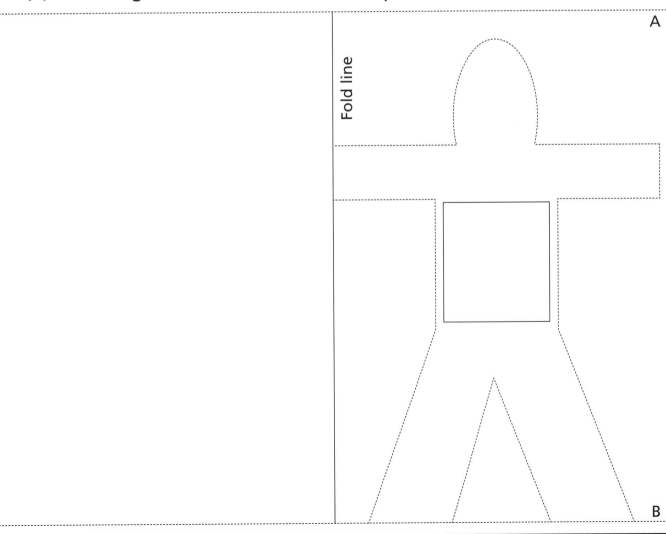

Accepting Personal Appearance

Indicators

- Understands there are aspects of personal appearance which can be changed and aspects which cannot be changed.
- Appreciates aspects of his/her own physical appearance which have been genetically inherited.
- Appreciates that the way people care for themselves affects their physical appearance.

Pre-Lesson Focus Discussion

Find or draw a selection of different-looking people as a stimulus for discussing similarities and differences in physical appearance.

Encourage the students to think about what the people illustrated can change about their appearance and what they cannot change.

Discuss where the unchangeable aspects of physical appearance came from—introduce the concept of heredity. Illustrate, using a family tree, how a particular feature might be passed down through the generations.

Using the Student Activity Sheet

1. Look at the cartoon at the top of the student activity page. Read the speech bubble and decide what Sam can and cannot change about himself.

2. Read the sentence in bold print and ask the students to predict what the two main reasons are for the way they look.

3. Read Reason 1 and direct the students to check the boxes in Question 1 to identify who they share physical traits with in their family.

4. Provide the students with a separate sheet of paper or allow them to use the back of the activity sheet to draw a picture of themselves, giving special attention to the physical traits they share with their family. Encourage the students to think about and reflect in their drawing what their body shape is; for example, tall, short, stocky, slight, lanky.

5. Direct the students to Reason 2. Have them suggest the types of things they could do to take care of themselves.

6. Read Question 3 with the students and allow them time to reflect upon an opportunity they had to care for something and how they managed the task. Ask them to write short answers to complete the question and then encourage them to share their experiences with the class.

7. Read Question 4 and allow the students to answer yes or no to each question as it is read. Encourage the students to assess from their answers whether or not they are taking good care of themselves.

Follow-Up Suggestions

Ask how exercise, sleep and eating good food (or the lack of all three) could affect a person's appearance.

Develop a class plan for taking care of themselves, including a fitness program and a "good foods" suggestion list.

Challenge the students to get their body in good shape by following the class plan.

Sensitivity Issues

Some students may be unaware of who one or both of their birthparents are, making it difficult to participate in Question 1. If the students are aware of this (some are not at this age), encourage them to move straight to Question 2, focusing on what they know about their physical appearance. Depending on the circumstances of the child, they may find comfort in imagining traits they might share with their birthparents.

Activity Links

Answers

Teacher check

I'm tall like my mom and have a smile like my uncle's.

There are two main reasons why you look the way you do.

Reason 1

You were made by mixing together part of your mom and part of your dad—so you look a little bit like both of them. People often look like other people in their family.

1. Check the circle if you look like any of these people in your family.

   O Mom   O Dad
   O Grandfather   O Grandmother
   O Aunt   O Uncle
   O Sister   O Brother

2. On a separate sheet of paper, draw a picture showing what you look like.

Reason 2

The way you look after yourself changes the way you look.

3. (a) Have you ever had to look after something special?

   Yes \ **No**

   (b) What did you look after?

   _____

   (c) How did you look after it?

   _____

   _____

   (d) What would have happened if you had not taken care of it?

   _____

4. Here are some ways we can look after ourselves. Answer "yes" or "no" to find out whether you are looking after yourself.

   (a) Do you eat good food?

   Yes \ **No**

   (b) Do you get enough exercise?

   Yes \ **No**

   (c) Do you go to bed early?

   Yes \ **No**

Eating the Right Food

Indicators

- Understands that what we put into our body affects our physical appearance.
- Understands that what we put into our body affects our health and well-being.
- Identifies foods which benefit physical health and well-being and foods which can be detrimental.

Pre-Lesson Focus Discussion

Show the students a picture of an overweight character from a nursery rhyme; for example, Old King Cole. Discuss why the students think he/she has that body shape.

Introduce the idea of eating enough food to keep your body moving – like putting fuel into a car. Ask the students to consider what would happen if someone kept putting more fuel in their body than they needed.

Using the Student Activity Sheet

1. Prepare one of each of the chimpanzees on the activity sheet by cutting and folding along the lines prior to the lesson. Show each of the figures to the students and ask them why they think they might look the way they do. How are they different? What have they done to look so different?

2. Open up the "stomach" of each chimpanzee and ask the students to suggest how many bananas and other foods that might be found.

3. Provide the students with activity sheets of their own and ask them to draw the number of bananas or other foods they think they would find in each chimpanzee's stomach.

4. When complete, encourage the students to share their ideas with the class. Allow the students time to add bananas and other foods to their own chimpanzee.

5. Show the students how to cut and fold their chimpanzees to make the two figures.

Follow-Up Suggestions

Have the students monitor what they eat in a day. Direct them to think about whether they are eating enough, just the right amount, or too much food for their body each day.

Make a healthy food collage using clippings from magazines and catalogs.

Make and eat healthy snacks as small-group activities.

Sensitivity Issues

Children who are overweight or underweight should not be made the "target" of this activity. Everyone has a different metabolism, affecting the amount he/she can eat and process. There is, therefore, no "right" quantity of food a student should be eating. Similarly, students will eat more during a growth spurt than they would normally and should not be made to feel guilty about the amount they eat. Be aware also of physiological problems that may cause abnormal weight gain or loss. The focus should remain on eating sensibly for their individual requirements.

Activity Links

Answers

Teacher check

1. How many bananas or other foods do you think these two funny chimpanzees eat to make them look the way they do? Draw food in each chimpanzee's stomach to show your answer.

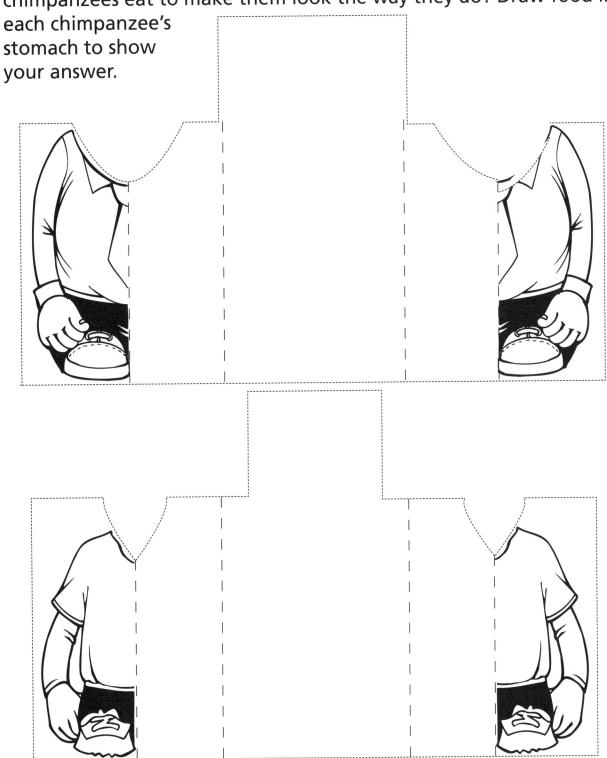

2. Cut around each of the chimpanzees. Fold along the dotted lines to make the body halves join in the middle. Draw faces for and color the two different chimpanzees you made.

Exercising

Indicators

- Understands that the food people eat provides energy to move their body.
- Understands that people need to be active to use up the energy they put into their bodies through eating food.
- Identifies activities which help to keep people's bodies active and healthy.
- Determines whether his/her own activity level is adequate.

Pre-Lesson Focus Discussion

Encourage the students to share examples of how they move their body. Use their suggestions to play games such as "Simon Says," or sing and act out simple songs such as "If You're Happy And You Know It."

Have the students consider what might happen if they never moved their bodies. What would happen to their body shape? What would happen to their muscles? What would happen to their bones?

Using the Student Activity Sheet

1. Look at the cartoon at the top of the student activity page. Ask the students what Billy is doing to move her body. The students might like to share their jump rope experiences or suggest jump rope games they know.

2. Read with the students the information in bold print about getting their bodies moving.

3. Brainstorm a list of ways to get their bodies moving.

4. Direct the students to the grid of words and pictures in Question 1 (a). Have the students suggest what is happening in the pictures and assist them to write an appropriate title for each where needed. Read the remaining words in the empty boxes and ask the students to draw a small cartoon to illustrate each.

5. Allow the students to choose an activity from the list brainstormed by the class or to think of their own activity to draw and label to complete Question 1 (b).

6. Encourage the students to think about how much activity they do and whether they consider their body to be "healthy and looking great" like Billy's. Read the text in bold print near the bottom of the page, then have them mark on the scale how much exercise they do to complete Question 2.

Follow-Up Suggestions

Set up some small-group physical activities to complete every morning. Encourage the students to suggest activities that would be suitable.

Make a graph of physical activities based on what the students think are the most fun ways to be active.

Sensitivity Issues

Children who are overweight or underweight should not be made the "target" of this activity. To encourage students, focus on the "fun" aspect of getting physical. Be aware that those with physical disabilities may require modified physical tasks in order to participate in pre-lesson and follow-up tasks.

Activity Links

Answers

Teacher check

Billy, Billy, turn around;
Billy, Billy, touch the ground.
We all saw what Billy did;
Now she is a healthy kid!
1, 2, 3, 4, 5, ...

When we eat food, it gives us energy to move our body. Moving your body can be lots of fun. What do you do to get your body moving?

1. (a) Finish the table by writing a word to match the picture or by drawing a picture to match the word.

    (b) Think of another way to move your body and draw and label it in the blank box.

_____   swimming   _____

bike riding

By using up our energy doing all these things, we can keep our body healthy and looking great. Billy exercises every day. She is healthy and happy.

2. How much exercise do you do?

| not enough | a little bit | some | a lot |

Sleep

Indicators

- Understands that people need to sleep every day.
- Understands people need sleep to grow, heal and build energy for the next day's activity.
- Assesses whether he or she is getting enough sleep.

Pre-Lesson Focus Discussion

Use a puppet or doll to demonstrate a nighttime routine to the students; for example, having a bath, brushing teeth, going to the bathroom, reading a book, saying goodnight. Alternatively, read the students a story about going to bed at night.

Encourage the students to share their nighttime routine with the class. Identify similarities and differences between the nighttime routines in different families.

Using the Student Activity Sheet

1. Look at the cartoon at the top of the student activity page. Ask the students why Billy might be feeling the way she is. What do they think happened just before she spoke to her mother? Do they think her mother is right about her being tired? Ask the students whether anyone has ever said that to them and how it made them feel.

2. Read the text in bold print describing why sleep is so important. Encourage the students to reiterate the key points in the text about why sleep is important; for example, to grow, to heal and to build energy for the next day.

3. Ask the students to share how they feel when they are tired. If appropriate, ask some students to role-play what they do or look like when they are tired.

4. Read Question 1 and the words in the quilt on Billy's bed with the students. Ask them to color the patches containing words that describe what they are like when they are tired.

5. Have the students follow your verbal instructions to role-play being tired, falling asleep, sleeping, and then waking up fresh and happy. Direct the students to Question 2 and have them draw their "fresh" face in the space provided.

6. Discuss what time is a good bedtime. Allow the students to decide and answer whether or not they get enough sleep and to draw hands on the clock to show their bedtime to complete Question 3.

Follow-Up Suggestions

Make individual clocks showing bedtime and wake-up time. Color the "sleeping" hours and encourage the students to count up how many hours of sleep they get every day.

Sensitivity Issues

In some households, bedtime is not a regularly held routine and students may suffer as a result. By encouraging all students to take responsibility for their bedtime and conduct a bedtime routine by themselves like a "big" person, those who are not regularly getting enough sleep can feel better equipped to take charge of their own sleeping habits.

Activity Links

My Special Jobs .... pp. 12–13
Why Do I Look the Way I Do? .... pp. 26–27
Getting Help When You're Feeling Bad .... pp. 62–63

Answers

Teacher check

Oh, Mom, nothing is working out right!

Billy, sometimes things seem worse than they are when you are tired. Why don't you get some sleep and see how you feel after that?

Billy's mom is wise. She knows that sleep is very important for kids. When you are asleep, your body grows, works on healing itself and gets a good rest, ready for the next day.

1. How do you feel when you are tired? Read the words on the patchwork quilt. Color in each of the patches that describes you when you are tired.

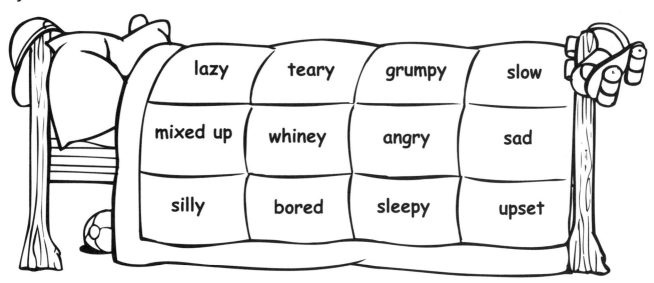

lazy	teary	grumpy	slow
mixed up	whiney	angry	sad
silly	bored	sleepy	upset

When we get a good night's sleep we feel much better.

2. Draw a face below to show how you feel after a good sleep.

3. (a) Do you think you get enough sleep? **Yes** \ **No**

(b) Draw hands on the clock to show what time you go to bed at night.

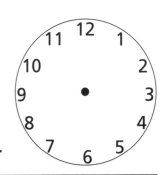

Playing and Having Fun

Indicators

- Appreciates that everyone needs to have fun.
- Understands that having fun helps people to be happy and feel good.
- Identifies the things he/she does to have fun with and without other people.

Pre-Lesson Focus Discussion

Play a game the students enjoy. Encourage them to have fun and enjoy a big laugh with their friends. Discuss how the activity made them feel. Did it cheer them up? Do they feel happier now than they did before?

Encourage the students to share a funny experience with their peers. Begin by sharing a funny story of your own, including funny actions or funny faces to make them laugh.

Discuss why we like funny things and what makes us laugh.

Using the Student Activity Sheet

1. Look at the cartoon at the top of the student activity page. Discuss what is happening in the cartoon and how Billy is feeling as she jumps rope.
2. Read the text in bold print and encourage the students to share their ideas about how people other than themselves might have fun. How do their parents have fun? Their siblings? What do they think teachers might do to have fun?
3. Read a short joke book or tell a joke to the class, encouraging them to have a big belly laugh. Ask the students what else makes them laugh and have them write their idea to answer Question 1.
4. Read the text in bold print to help introduce the idea of having fun by yourself as well as having fun with other people. Brainstorm to list some ideas for fun things they can do by themselves. Allow the students to draw in the space provided something they have fun doing by themselves.
5. Discuss with whom the students most enjoy having fun. What do they enjoy doing with this person/these people? The students can then draw a picture of something they have fun doing with other people in the space provided to complete Question 2.
6. Ask the students whether they consider themselves to be happy and whether or not they feel like they need other people to help them have fun. Challenge the students to think of something fun they could do today. Use these reflections to complete Question 3.

Follow-Up Suggestions

Encourage the students to follow through on their suggestion for a fun activity from Question 3 later that day.

Make a class "fun" book full of the students' ideas on how to have fun, jokes and fun games the students could play. Use the book as a resource during any "free time" opportunities the students may have.

Sensitivity Issues

Ensure that any "funny" stories the students tell are not at someone else's expense and do not hurt anyone's feelings. If such a situation arises, use the opportunity to demonstrate that not all things are funny to all people and that we need to be considerate of other people's feelings. Take note of students who constantly use themselves as "the joke" as this may reflect issues causing poor self-esteem which can later be addressed.

Activity Links

Answers

Teacher check

Everyone needs to have fun sometimes—even moms, dads and teachers! Having fun helps you to think about happy things and to feel good. It helps you to be a happy person—and happy people make great friends. Having a big laugh is good for you ... Try it!

1. Write something that makes you have a big laugh.

_____

_____

The easiest way to have fun is to play. You can play and have fun by yourself or with other people.

2. Draw pictures showing how you have fun ...

by yourself.   with other people.

3. (a) Are you a happy person?   (b) How will you have fun today?

Yes	No

_____

_____

_____

Caring for Others

Indicators

- Appreciates that the way people behave demonstrates how much they care about others.
- Differentiates between behaviors that are caring and those that are not.
- Identifies the types of caring behavior he/she appreciates in others.
- Identifies the caring behaviors he/she demonstrates towards others and what he/she could do to become a more caring person.

Pre-Lesson Focus Discussion

Share a package of stickers among the students in the class. Discuss whether the gesture was a caring one. Discuss whether the stickers were shared fairly and whether everyone feels cared for.

Have the students suggest ways we can care about other people.

Discuss people who may need a particular type or amount of care.

Using the Student Activity Sheet

1. Role-play forgetting a lunch and being very hungry. Have the students suggest how they could respond in a caring way. Direct the students to the cartoon at the top of the student activity page and discover what theDella in the cartoon did to care for Billy.
2. Read the text in bold print, challenging the students to think about their own actions and whether or not they are caring people.
3. Direct the students to the boxes with the cartoons showing different types of behaviors. Discuss each briefly and ask the students to indicate which people they would most like to be around. Encourage the students to give verbal reasons for their choices.
4. Read Question 2 and the sentences in each box around the person. Have the students draw a line from the person to each of the behaviors he/she demonstrates with others. Stress that they should be honest in their response.
5. The students can then share a caring behavior they feel they are particularly good at with the class and suggest something they could do more often in the future to demonstrate that they care about other people.

Follow-Up Suggestions

Suggest scenarios in which someone needs help for the students to role-play and respond to in a caring way.

Give students "Caring and Sharing" awards for caring behaviors they demonstrate toward their peers.

Sensitivity Issues

Address problems between students from a "caring" perspective. Ask the students how they could demonstrate more caring behavior towards the person with whom they are having a problem. Students will best learn caring behavior when it is consistently demonstrated towards them by adults. Take care to demonstrate the types of caring, tolerant behavior you expect of them in your dealings with students. In this way, a safe and caring environment can be created within which the students can develop these skills.

Activity Links

Answers

Teacher check

What kind of person are you? Do you share toys with other students? Do you take care of other people when they need help? These are some of the kind things we can do to be a good person.

1. Check the boxes that show the kind of person you would like to be around.

2. (a) Imagine the person below is you. Use a red pencil to draw a line from you to each of the boxes that say a kind thing you do.

I share toys.

I say kind things.

I help others.

I have fun.

I invite people to play with me.

I say sorry if I hurt someone.

(b) Draw a blue line from you to the boxes that are left. See if you can remember to do these things next time you play.

Keeping Safe From Harmful Things

Indicators

- Understands that people are responsible for their own actions.
- Recognizes warning labels and responds with caution.
- Predicts the consequences of unsafe behaviors.

Pre-Lesson Focus Discussion

Provide a number of household items displaying "Keep out of reach of children," poison symbols, or warnings. Discuss the dangers associated with each item and the importance of displaying such warnings.

Encourage the students to share experiences where they have encountered or heard about people who have not followed the rules. Ask the students how the situation could have been prevented.

Using the Student Activity Sheet

1. Look at the cartoon at the top of the student activity page with the students and discuss what is happening. Why is Sam trying to get into the cupboard? What might be in the cupboard? What might happen to him if he does get in? How could he avoid disaster?

2. Read the text in bold print following the cartoon and direct the students' attention back to the items brought from home.

3. Look at the five unfinished words in Question 1. Have the students sound out each word and add an initial consonant to complete them and reveal things that could be dangerous to children.

4. Students draw a picture for Question 2 showing how something from the list can be dangerous; for example, a fire could start from playing with matches.

5. Read the text in bold print at the bottom of the page and discuss Sam's actions. Allow the students to respond to Question 3 independently as a result of this and earlier discussion.

Follow-Up Suggestions

Make a class collage of warning labels, pictures of dangerous products and poison symbols. Encourage the students to be on the lookout at the supermarket for unsafe products.

Have the students write short statements about how they keep safe and make a sign to demonstrate their statement. For example, "I keep safe by not playing with matches," accompanied by a picture of matches with a red diagonal line through it.

Sensitivity Issues

The use of medicine or needles may be a necessary part of daily life for some students. Clarify safe and unsafe usage of such items if necessary.

Activity Links

Answers

1. (a) matches   (b) cleaners   (c) medicine
   (d) poison   (e) knives
2. Teacher check
3. Answers will vary

> I wonder what Mom keeps up in this cabinet? I wonder why she doesn't want me to have it? I can nearly reach...

There are some things that have a warning label that means "Keep out of reach of children."

1. Fill in the missing letters to complete things which could be harmful to children.

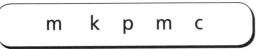

   m k p m c

   (a) ＿＿＿ a t c h e s

   (b) ＿＿＿ l e a n e r s

   (c) ＿＿＿ e d i c i n e

   (d) ＿＿＿ o i s o n

   (e) ＿＿＿ n i v e s

2. Draw a picture showing how something from the list can be dangerous.

Sam is doing something very silly and wrong. He is not taking care of himself.

3. (a) Sam thinks he is being clever. Do you? Yes \ No

   (b) Write what might happen to Sam if he gets into the cupboard full of dangerous things.

   _____

   _____

   _____

Self-Image

Indicators

- Differentiates between his/her public image and self-image.
- Understands that self-image is a combination of physical and emotional self-perception.
- Willingly shares opinions about self.

Pre-Lesson Focus Discussion

Ask a student to stand in front of a mirror and tell the class what he/she sees. Encourage him/her to give a physical description of his/her image to the class. Discuss whether what the student sees is the same as what the rest of the class sees. Ask the class to suggest things about the student that cannot be seen in the mirror to introduce the idea that a whole person's image is not just what they see but also what others have learned about them and feel about them.

Discuss whether what other people think of us and what we think of ourselves are the same thing. Encourage the students to think about times when this might not be the case.

Using the Student Activity Sheet

1. Direct the students to Question 1 on the student activity page. Read parts (a) and (b) and allow the students to indicate their response for each.
2. Draw a large mirror on the board for the students to see and write examples of words that describe you. Ask the students to identify words that describe what you are like on the outside and underline them in green. Similarly, demonstrate how to identify and underline in purple the words describing what you are like on the inside.
3. Allow the students time to complete the task independently. They may choose to share their ideas with the class; however, this information should be provided on a voluntary basis only.
4. Have the students reflect upon Question 3 and determine whether or not other people know the things they have written about themselves.

Follow-Up Suggestions

Conduct a "sharing" morning, encouraging the students to share something about themselves that they think not many people in the class would know. Use the information from the sharing morning to create a class big book titled "Did You Know?"

Encourage the students to write short positive statements about why they like someone in the class. It may help to provide each student with a person to write about to avoid some students missing out.

Sensitivity Issues

Self-image is very personal and not something which is comfortably shared by most. Though clarifying self-image may help many students to understand themselves and why they feel the way they do, any sharing of feelings about self must be voluntary and treated with the utmost respect. Students should be instructed not to comment upon other people's opinions of themselves or to repeat personal information shared by their peers.

Activity Links

Answers

Teacher check

1. Answer these questions about yourself.

    (a) What do you think of yourself? I am | **good** \ **okay** \ **bad** |.

    (b) Would you like to be friends with someone like you?
       | **Yes** \ **No** |

2. Write words in the mirror to describe yourself. Use a green pencil to underline words describing what you are like on the outside. Use a purple pencil to underline words describing what you are like on the inside.

My name:

3. Do you think other people know all these things about you?
    | **Yes** \ **No** |

Perceptions of Others

Indicators

- Learns about how others perceive him/her.
- Identifies and offers positive feedback to peers.

Pre-Lesson Focus Discussion

Play a "circle" game that encourages the students to make positive comments about other class members. For example, have a student roll a ball to another student across the circle. The student who receives the ball must say something positive about the person who has just rolled it. The receiver then rolls the ball to another class member and so on.

Using the Student Activity Sheet

1. Look at the cartoon at the top of the page with the students. Ask them to reflect upon what Sam likes about Della. Discuss whether Della would know this from his comment and how Della would have felt to receive such positive words from her friend.

2. Read the activity instructions with the students. Discuss what it would feel like if no one came and wrote something in their shapes. Encourage the students to be aware of people who look left out and to make an effort to include everyone in the class, even if they are not people they know well.

3. Allow the students time to move around the room and write positive comments on each other's activity sheets.

4. After ample time has been given to complete the task, students can read the comments to themselves.

Follow-Up Suggestions

Have the students identify three people to praise in some way during the day. Ask the students to write down the three they have in mind and to check them off when they have achieved their goal. Encourage the students to pick three people they normally would not spend much time with or who they think would really appreciate hearing something positive about themselves.

Sensitivity Issues

Students who are more introverted may have difficulty approaching other students to complete this task. Attempt to compensate for this by modeling how to approach someone not well known and discussing how being included feels compared to being left out. Take the opportunity to monitor and model inclusive behavior. It could even be suggested that someone's ability to include others may be a positive trait to write about.

Activity Links

What I'm Like On the Inside ....pp. 8–9

Let's Celebrate! ....pp. 20–21

Being My Best ....pp. 24–25

Sharing and Caring ....pp. 36–37

Saying Positive Things ....pp. 72–73

Friends Chain ....pp. 76–77

Accepting People As They Are........................pp. 86–87

Can I Play? ....pp. 94–95

Answers

Teacher check

1. Write your name in the scroll in the middle of the page.

2. Give your page to someone in the class to write something he or she likes about you in one of the shapes. Don't forget to write something you like about him or her in one of his or her shapes.

3. Give your paper to other people in your class until all of the shapes have been written in.

4. Read all the great things people like about you.

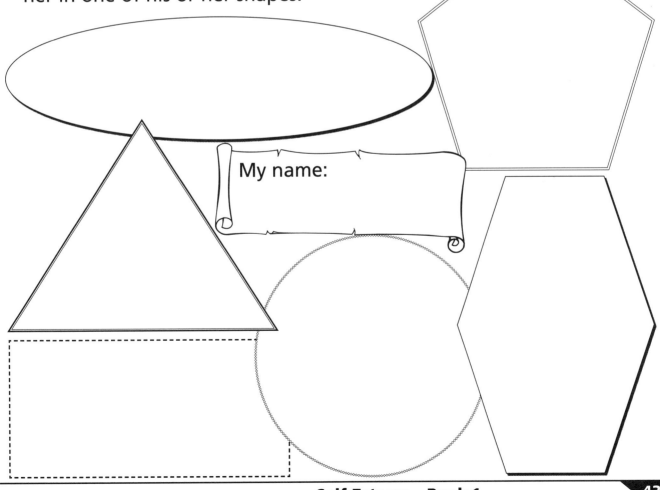

My name:

Creating a Positive Image

Indicators

- Identifies behaviors that are effective in building a positive image.
- Attempts to identify what is popular among his/her peers.
- Understands that pretending to be like someone else is not "cool."

Pre-Lesson Focus Discussion

Discuss what is meant by the word "cool." Brainstorm to list cool behaviors and personality traits.

Ask students to role-model what they think cool looks or sounds like. Discuss whether trying to be like someone else is cool. How does it feel to have to try to behave in a way that is not like you all the time. Is this cool?

Review what makes someone cool, trying to avoid the common stereotyping associated with the term.

Using the Student Activity Sheet

1. Look at the cartoon at the top of the student activity page. Ask the students if they think the girl on the left is cool and to give reasons for their answers. Discuss why they think Sam holds the opinion that she is not cool.

2. Read the text in bold print with the students and clarify what is meant by being yourself. Discuss the benefits of being yourself—how does it make life easier? Why is being yourself cool?

3. Direct the students to the four ice cubes at the bottom of the page. Read the cool behaviors in each of the ice cubes and discuss why these things are cool. Challenge the students to think about whether or not they are cool and how they could become "more cool" without trying to be like someone else; for example, anyone can be friendly and laugh regardless of their looks or personality.

4. Allow the students time to draw themselves in each of the ice cubes doing the cool things written in them.

Follow-Up Suggestions

Develop a set of class rules based on what is "cool" and what is "uncool." For example, "damaging other people's things is uncool" or "trying hard at school is cool."

Encourage the students to think about "staying cool" when sorting out problems and disagreements.

Sensitivity Issues

When discussing cool and uncool behavior, be careful not to use students in the school as examples of "what not to do." Also, though students should be encouraged to be themselves, they should be guided towards being the best version of themselves. Guidance should be positive to assist them to behave in the most socially acceptable and effective way they can.

Before the students complete the activity, teachers could discuss that although it is "cool" to make friends, it can also be difficult. This may help those students who have few or no friends for a range of reasons.

Activity Links

Answers

Teacher check

Some people do and say some silly things to try to be cool—just like this girl. She is being bossy and showing off. That's not cool. The most important thing you can do to be cool is just be yourself! Don't pretend to be someone else.

Draw a picture of yourself doing each of the cool things written near the ice cubes.

Cool people make friends.

Cool people laugh and have fun.

Cool people are nice to others.

Cool people look after themselves by keeping fit and clean.

Feelings

Indicators

- Recognizes that all people experience a range of emotions.
- Understands that people have different feelings in response to different situations.
- Identifies own feelings in response to given situations.

Pre-Lesson Focus Discussion

Have the students share how they feel at the beginning of the lesson. Discuss whether anything happened prior to the lesson for them to feel a certain way.

Discuss different types of feelings we can experience and how we can tell when a person is feeling a certain way. Ask the students to alter their facial expression and body language to reflect some of the feelings suggested.

Using the Student Activity Sheet

1. Direct the students to the student activity page. Read each of the sentences in Question 1 and allow the students to finish the sentences with suitable feelings.

2. Read Question 2 and have the students follow the instructions together to complete the "feelings" strip. Read the sentence "I feel ..." for each of the four possibilities provided on the strip.

3. Tell a range of short stories or explain simple scenarios and ask the students to select a feeling response for each situation. The students may also suggest different feeling responses for some scenarios. These could be listed on the board and used to make new feelings strips. Encourage the students to give reasons for their response. Suggested story topics could include:

   - Walking a pet dog.
   - Receiving a special gift.
   - Someone giving you a compliment.
   - Feeling left out or not allowed to join in.
   - Parents or friends arguing.
   - Someone telling mean stories about you.
   - Going to a really special place.
   - First day of summer vacation.

   - Receiving a hug from someone special.
   - Spending quality time with a good friend.
   - A friend moving away.
   - Feeling sick.
   - Someone ruining something precious.
   - Someone hurting you or calling you names.
   - Going to a birthday party.
   - Eating your favorite meal.

Follow-Up Suggestions

Allow the students to make up short skits and have the audience use their feelings strips to indicate how a certain character might be feeling at different times.

Read books which address emotional issues and encourage the students to identify feelings the characters in the book are experiencing.

Sensitivity Issues

Feelings and emotions are not representative of who a person is, but rather, are a reflection of the circumstances in which he/she exists at a given time. Refrain from labeling people as being, for example, "sad" or "angry," as these labels can serve to perpetuate an emotional state due to expectation rather than as a logical emotional response.

Activity Links

Answers

1. (a) hungry
   (b) tired
   (c) happy
2. Teacher check

Everyone has feelings. How are you feeling right now? How do you think the other people in your class feel?

I have the feeling that this is going to be fun.

1. Read the sentences and write in the missing words.

   (a) When I need to eat, I feel h __ __ __ __ __.

   (b) When I need sleep, I feel t __ __ __ __.

   (c) When I laugh, I feel h __ __ __ __.

2. (a) Draw faces to match the words on the "feelings" strip.

   (b) Cut around the feelings strip and "I feel" card.

   (c) Cut slits in the "I feel" card along the dotted lines.

   (d) Thread the feelings strip through the "I feel" card.

   (e) Listen to stories from your teacher and change the face shown to show how the story makes you feel.

happy.

sad.

angry.

excited.

I feel

Reasons for Feelings

Indicators

- Understands that feelings change.
- Understands that people can control the way they respond to their feelings.
- Identifies means to help himself/herself feel better.

Pre-Lesson Focus Discussion

Ask the students to share situations where they have felt sad or upset. Have them describe what led them to have these feelings and whether the feelings lasted for a long time or a short time. Ask the students whether they felt there was anything they could do when they were upset to change how they felt.

Discuss the types of things that cheer them up when they are feeling down. Identify which of these things they can do to help themselves and which require the helping hand of another person.

Using the Student Activity Sheet

1. Look at the cartoon at the top of the student activity page and use it to readdress the idea of how a friend can help someone feel better.

2. Allow the students time to draw a picture that shows a situation where they became upset. They can then complete the sentence "I feel upset when ..." Some students may need assistance from a teacher or assistant to simplify their situation into a sentence.

3. Allow the students to draw what they did to feel better in the second box and complete the sentence "I feel happy again when ..." Where appropriate, encourage the students to share their before and after stories with the class.

4. Read the text in bold print, then the ideas suggested in the boxes in Question 2. The students can reflect upon each suggestion and color one or more boxes describing what they do to cheer themselves up.

Follow-Up Suggestions

The period after playtime is often a bustling frenzy of discussion of the events of the break. Give the students the opportunity to share their playtime experiences and reflect upon how they made them feel. Encourage the students to share stories about people who were upset during the break and what they did to try to cheer them up.

Sensitivity Issues

Not all "upsets" can be healed quickly and should be given a proportionate response. Be prepared for the possibility of students disclosing sensitive information in regard to what upsets them. All disclosures should be taken seriously and should, if necessary, go through the appropriate channels as outlined in the school's child protection policy.

Activity Links
Answers

Teacher check

1. Draw pictures in the boxes to show what makes you feel upset and what helps you feel happy again. Finish the sentences.

(a) I feel upset when

_____

_____

(b) I feel happy again when

_____

_____

There are many different things you can do to help yourself when you are upset.

2. Color what you do to feel better when you are upset.

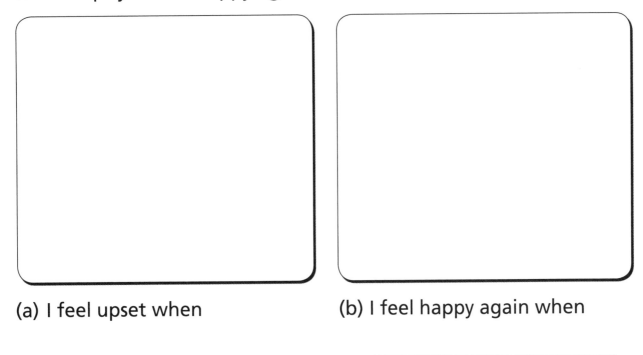

| cry | get a hug | run around outside | play with friends |

| read a book | other _____ |

Personal Feelings

Indicators

- Understands that people can feel different emotions about themselves.
- Identifies personality traits and feelings that represent himself/herself.

Pre-Lesson Focus Discussion

Introduce the idea of having feelings about ourselves. Do you like who you are? Do some of the things you do or have done make you feel bad about yourself?

Explain that the way we feel about ourselves can change depending upon what we do and what we experience. Have the students discuss the types of things which may lead us not to feel good about ourselves; for example, if we are mean or tease others.

Using the Student Activity Sheet

1. Read the text in bold print at the top of the student activity page. Have the students reflect upon the questions posed and respond voluntarily if they wish.
2. Direct the students to the figure outlined on the page and ask them to draw their face onto the person.
3. Read the words at the bottom of the page. Have the students cut them out and choose those which best represent how they feel about themselves and their personality traits.
4. The students can then glue the appropriate patches onto the figure's overalls, discarding the remaining patches, and color in their "person."
5. Allow the students to share with their peers the patches they felt best described them.

Follow-Up Suggestions

Use the people created during the activity to make a display showing how the people in the class are alike and different, promoting acceptance and tolerance of others.

Note students who are struggling with self-esteem and take steps to build a more positive environment in which they feel safe and encouraged.

Sensitivity Issues

People with poor self-esteem usually believe they have good reason to feel the way they do about themselves. Students who appear to be suffering from poor self-esteem should be addressed with compassion and understanding in combination with some strategies to enable them to take charge of their feelings and become resilient in difficult situations. The activities within this book can be carefully selected by teachers according to the students' needs and will equip them with coping strategies and address many of the issues faced by school-aged students.

Activity Links

Answers

Teacher check

People who like themselves are happy and have fun. What sort of person are you? Do you like who you are?

1. (a) Draw your face on the figure.

   (b) Choose and color five "patches" from the bottom of the page that have words describing the kind of person you are.

   (c) Cut out the patches you colored and glue them onto the overalls.

My name:

shy	rough and tough	happy	angry	good friend	sad	quiet
nice to people	lonely	chatterbox	fun	mean	caring	try hard

Feelings – Card Game

Indicators

- Recognizes a wide variety of feelings and emotions.
- Plays, with peers, an interactive card game about feelings.
- Independently plays a card game about feelings.

Pre-Lesson Focus Discussion

Introduce a pre-prepared set of "Feeling Snappy" cards to the students. Use the images on the cards as flashcards to familiarize them with the different emotions and feelings included in the set.

Discuss the types of games that could be played with the cards. Suggestions could include "Concentration," "Snap" and "Fish." Review how each of these games is played.

Using the Student Activity Sheet

1. Provide each student with an activity sheet with the "Feeling Snappy" playing cards. The cards will be more durable if the activity is photocopied onto light card stock. The students can color the faces on each of the cards using matching colors if desired.
2. Have the students cut out the playing cards and write their initials on the back.
3. Provide them with an envelope or plastic baggie to keep their set of cards in.
4. Allow the students to play with their cards, either independently or in a small group.

Follow-Up Suggestions

Sets of "Feeling Snappy" can be made available to the students during free-time activities.

Review concepts such as sharing and taking turns and discuss why manners are necessary when playing games with others.

Sensitivity Issues

Be aware of students who may be left out of small-group card-playing activities. If necessary, form groups randomly to ensure inclusiveness.

Activity Links

1. Color and cut out the cards.
2. Use the cards to play "snap" or "memory" games.

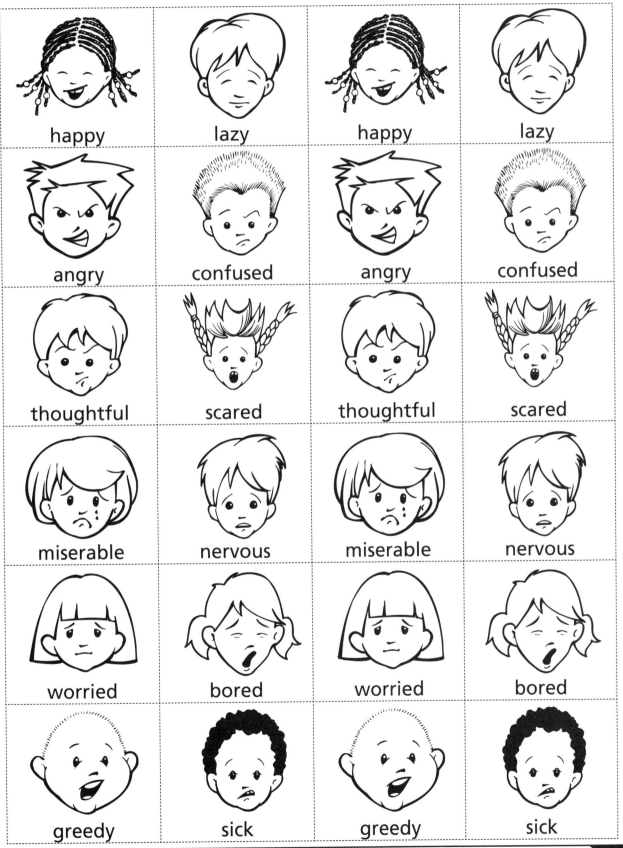

happy	lazy	happy	lazy
angry	confused	angry	confused
thoughtful	scared	thoughtful	scared
miserable	nervous	miserable	nervous
worried	bored	worried	bored
greedy	sick	greedy	sick

Creating Positive Approaches

Indicators

- Identifies things that make him/her feel good.
- Understands people have a responsibility to help themselves feel good.
- Identifies a way he/she could cheer up when feeling bad.

Pre-Lesson Focus Discussion

Have the students close their eyes and imagine the happiest place in the world. Imagine what it looks like, feels like and smells like. Offer suggestions to prompt their imagination; for example, Is it warm? Cool? What are you wearing? What can you see?

Encourage the students to share their imaginary happy place with the group.

Using the Student Activity Sheet

1. Look at the cartoon at the top of the student activity page. Ask the students what they like to do to make themselves feel better.

2. Challenge the students to think about a happy place and activity they enjoy. Allow them to write simple answers in response to Question 1. The students can share their ideas if they wish.

3. Direct the students to use the space provided to draw an image that describes the place and activity they have in mind. They can also include the people they might like to be with, if any.

4. Ask the students whether they think doing what they drew would cheer them up if they were feeling bad. Then have them respond to answer Question 3.

5. Suggest to the students that they could try out the activity next time they were feeling bad to see if it improves the way they feel.

Follow-Up Suggestions

Combine the students' activity pages to create a "Cheer Up" book for them to refer to for ideas when they are feeling bad.

Have the students write a description of their happy place to accompany the pictures they drew.

Sensitivity Issues

Finding a happy thing to do is a great strategy for helping students find relief from bad feelings but will not necessarily solve their problem, depending on its nature. Students should also be equipped with conflict resolution strategies to help them deal with problems and learn to be responsible for resolving issues.

Activity Links

Answers

Teacher check

1. What makes you happy?

    (a) Where are you happiest?

    _____

    _____

    _____

    (b) What do you do there?

    _____

    _____

    _____

    (c) Whom do you do it with? _____

    _____

2. Draw what makes you happy, using the answers you wrote to help you.

3. Do you think doing what you drew could cheer
    you up if you were feeling bad?   Yes \ No

Next time you feel bad, try cheering yourself up by doing what you drew.

Understanding and Managing Anger

Indicators

- Understands that anger can cause people to behave in unacceptable ways.
- Identifies bad things which can result from angry behavior.
- Accepts that people can control the way they respond to angry feelings.

Pre-Lesson Focus Discussion

Discuss what angry people look like. Have the students suggest physical characteristics of an angry person and draw these on a figure outline for the students to view. Ask the students whether anger makes them look good. How would they feel if someone saw them looking like the angry person drawn?

Discuss what anger feels like. Encourage the students to share experiences they have had when they have felt angry. What did they feel like doing? What did they do? Do they have any regrets about the way they behaved?

Using the Student Activity Sheet

1. Look at the cartoon at the top of the student activity page. Have the students suggest what might have happened to make Della so angry and to predict what they think is going to happen next. Draw attention to Billy's response to Della's anger and have the students share how they have felt when confronted by an angry person.

2. Read the text in bold and discuss why we might need to "be careful" when we become angry.

3. Read Question 1 as a class and allow the students to answer. They may share their experiences if they wish.

4. Direct the students to Question 2 and read the three bad things suggested that can happen when people get angry. Allow the students time to draw a picture to represent each of these things.

5. Read the text in bold print about having a plan for "cooling down" when they are angry. Reiterate why cooling down is important. Discuss whether cooling down would be an easy thing for Della to do. Explain that we have to be responsible when we become angry and take charge. Encourage the students to suggest ways they could cool down when they are angry.

6. Allow the students time to draw a picture representing what they consider would be the best way to cool down if they were to become angry.

Follow-Up Suggestions

Compile a list of "cool down" strategies for the students to refer to and suggest students who are having angry feelings refer to the list and choose a way to cool down to help them regain control.

Sensitivity Issues

Anger usually results from a conflict involving another person or persons. Cooling down is the first step to resolving the issue and will allow students to be more responsive in their efforts to discuss, offer sensible solutions and resolve the conflict. Be aware of the possibility that students who demonstrate extreme behavior when angry may be acting out a response they have witnessed at home or in another familiar environment and may themselves be at risk.

Activity Links

Answers

Teacher check

Everyone has feelings and everyone gets angry sometimes. We can do our best not to let ourselves get angry—but if we do, we need to be careful.

1. Have you ever felt really angry about something? **Yes** \ **No**

    What happened? _____

    _____

2. When people get angry, bad things can happen. Draw a picture for each of these bad things that come from angry feelings.

    (a) someone could be hurt (b) someone's feelings could be hurt (c) someone's things could be damaged

When we get angry, we need to have a plan for how to cool down, so we don't do anything bad.

3. Draw what you do to cool down.

Losing Someone Special

Indicators

- Recognizes that losing a friend, relative, or special person can make people feel sad.
- Shares his/her feelings about losing a special person in his/her life.
- Identifies people who are important to him/her.

Pre-Lesson Focus Discussion

Share an experience you have had of a close friend or relative moving away. Talk about all the great things you used to do together and how much you valued the time you had together. Ask the students to predict how you felt when the person moved away and how your behavior might have changed.

Encourage the students to share their own stories about losing someone who was special to them. Suggest that sometimes we are the ones who leave and discuss how this scenario might make us feel.

Using the Student Activity Sheet

1. Introduce the student activity sheet by looking at Billy and reading the text in bold print.
2. Have the students suggest some of the special people they have in their life, both friends and family. Ask the students to draw a picture of four of these people and write their names underneath.
3. Ask the students to choose one of these special people and imagine he/she has to go away. Encourage them to explain how they would feel if that ever happened and then draw a picture of themselves showing an expression which describes how they would feel.
4. Discuss how we could be a good friend to someone who has lost someone special. How would we want to be treated under the same circumstances?
5. Read the words and phrases describing things people might do if they lost a special person from their life. To complete Question 2, ask the students to circle the things they would do if they were in that situation.

Follow-Up Suggestions

Make a class photo album of the students in the class. Include all the things which are special about each person. Continue to update the album as new students arrive and allow the class to visit the album in quiet reading time to remember students who may have left during the year.

Have the students write a "memory story" about someone they once knew well who is now not in their life.

Sensitivity Issues

Be aware that students from split families may be experiencing considerable grief at the loss of one or both of their parents. These students, and those dealing with a death in the family, should not be forced to share personal details about their situation with the class. If the students wish to discuss these things with you, arrange a more private follow-up time with you or a counselor when the student can share thoughts and feelings safely.

Activity Links

Answers

Teacher check

When a special person leaves our life, we can feel very sad.

1. Who are some of the special people in your life? Draw a face in each box and write the person's name underneath.

_____ _____ _____ _____

2. (a) Choose one of the people you drew and imagine he or she has to move away. Draw your face in the mirror to show how you would feel.

(b) Circle what you would do if you lost one of the special people in your life.

cry

be quiet

pretend to be happy

forget about him/her

look at photos of him/her

write to him/her

remember him/her

try to cheer up

Being Sick or Unable to Join In

Indicators

- Understands there are some sicknesses that are contagious and some that are not.

- Understands that when a person is sick with something contagious he/she cannot play with others.

- Identifies feelings associated with not being able to join in with friends.

Pre-Lesson Focus Discussion

Discuss sickness and how it can be spread from one person to another. Address the importance of keeping clean and living a healthy lifestyle to help prevent becoming sick.

Allow the students to share their experiences of being sick, what they were and were not allowed or able to do while they were sick. Discuss how being sick can make you feel.

Challenge the students to think of health problems that could prevent them from doing the things they want to do but are not transferred from one person to another. Have the students imagine they are in a situation like this and to share how they think it would make them feel.

Using the Student Activity Sheet

1. Discuss the cartoon at the top of the student activity sheet. Ask the students what they think Billy is thinking about and feeling.

2. Read the text in bold print about being sick. Have the students read and answer Question 1 to help them relate to the idea of being sick and the feelings accompanying the situation.

3. Review the concept of sickness being spread from one person to another and use the cartoon in Question 2 to illustrate how this might happen. Have the students draw tissues on the noses of four of the little goats in the picture they think have caught the cold.

4. Read the text in bold print which follows and discuss why it is so important to stay away from others when they are sick.

5. Introduce the idea of sicknesses which cannot be spread from one person to another; for example, asthma. Think about whether or not people with these sicknesses should be allowed to come to school and be around other people. Encourage the students to give reasons for their viewpoint.

6. Allow the students to complete Question 3 (a) to describe how they would treat a person with a noncontagious health problem. Brainstorm to list ideas for games you could play with a person who is sick in this way, and have the students choose one or two to use as their answer to 3 (b).

Follow-Up Suggestions

Invite a person with a noncontagious health problem to come to speak with the students. Discuss issues such as acceptance and joining in with others.

Review rules for maintaining good hygiene; for example, washing hands after going to the bathroom and before eating, covering our mouth when we cough.

Sensitivity Issues

While it is important to understand that controlling the spread of sickness will prevent others from becoming sick unnecessarily, it is equally important to recognize that sickness is not a person's identity. For example, just because someone has a sickness does not make him/her "the sick kid" or "sickly." Be particularly conscious of students who have ongoing illnesses which are not contagious, such as asthma and diabetes, so they are not made to feel uncomfortable and their peers do not develop unnecessary fears about their illness.

Activity Links

Answers

Teacher check

Being sick is not much fun. Often it means you can't join in and play with friends.

1. (a) How do you feel when you are sick?

happy	bored	lonely	sad

other _____

   (b) Why do you feel like that? _____

Did you know there are different kinds of sickness? Some people become sick by being around other sick people. Sicknesses like colds are spread this way.

2. This little goat has spread his cold to four of his friends. Draw tissues on the four you think have his cold.

It is important to stay at home and not pass on sickness to our friends. Wait until you feel better.

Some people are sick with diseases that cannot be passed on to other people.

3. (a) Should you play with someone with a sickness you can not catch?

Yes	No

   (b) What games could you play with him/her? _____

   _____

   _____

Talking to Responsible Adults

Indicators

- Understands that sometimes we need to ask for help.
- Identifies situations when he/she may need help from an adult.
- Identifies a pool of responsible adults he/she could go to for help.

Pre-Lesson Focus Discussion

Share experiences when the students have needed help from an adult. Challenge the students to think about why they chose that adult and whether or not any other adult could have helped them in their situation.

Discuss what is meant by the word "trust." How do you know when someone can be trusted? What kinds of things can you talk about to someone you trust? Who are the people they feel they can trust in their lives?

Using the Student Activity Sheet

1. Look at the cartoon at the top of the student activity page. Ask the students whether they have ever felt like Billy and why they think she might be feeling so bad. Why is her mother advising her not to give up?

2. Read the text in bold print about things that can cause us to feel bad. Take time to discuss examples of each thing suggested. Ask the students, "How do people let us down? What wrong things might someone make us do? Why would someone tell lies?"

3. Have the students hold up a hand and think of a trusted adult they feel they could go to for help for each of their fingers. Allow the students to draw pictures of their five trusted adults on the petals of the flower.

4. The students can then write their name onto the middle of the flower and cut out their flower along the dotted line. Encourage the students to keep their flower somewhere that will remind them that help is there whenever they need it.

Follow-Up Suggestions

Use the flowers to create a class display titled "These People Can Help Me Feel Better." Encourage the students to use bright happy colors to color their flowers.

Invite a local police officer to come and talk to the students about situations when they should get help and to familiarize the students with the role police play in helping and protecting people in the community.

Sensitivity Issues

Questioning during this activity may prompt students to disclose sensitive information in order to get help. All disclosures should be taken seriously and, if necessary, should go through the appropriate channels as outlined in the school's child protection policy. If a situation arises where the student reveals information during part of a class discussion, encourage the student to see you privately after the lesson.

Activity Links

Answers

Teacher check

Things are not always good in our life. People can let us down, make us do things that are wrong, or even tell lies. If you are feeling bad and need help, you have to ask for it.

Draw five people in the petals of the flower whom you know you could ask for help. Write your name in the center of the flower.

These People Will Help Me

Asking for help is the right thing to do.

Being Happy Alone

Indicators

- Understands that being alone is different from feeling lonely.
- Appreciates that being alone can be enjoyable.
- Identifies activities which are best enjoyed alone.

Pre-Lesson Focus Discussion

Have the students lie down in their own space, not touching any other student and relaxing as they listen to you describe a peaceful, quiet place where they are completely on their own. Use a soothing voice and aim to make the description as pleasant and relaxing an experience as possible. When finished, ask the students to sit up and share how "escaping" to the quiet place made them feel.

Discuss other places they could go to be alone. Consider the types of things they could do there on their own that they couldn't do or enjoy if surrounded by other people.

Using the Student Activity Sheet

1. Look at the cartoon at the top of the student activity page. Share ideas about how Billy is feeling in the cartoon.

2. Read the text in bold print comparing the difference between being alone and being lonely.

3. Read Question 1 and brainstorm to list fun or relaxing things the students can do on their own. Have them select several ideas or use ideas of their own to write on the book to complete Question 1.

4. Discuss the students' favorite things to do on their own. Direct them to the circles at the bottom of the page. Encourage the students to think of their favorite "alone" activity and draw themselves doing that thing in the circle on the left of the page. They can then complete the sentence on the circle on the right, "When I am alone, I like to ... ."

5. When complete, demonstrate how to cut out, glue back to back and attach string to create a personal ornament for display.

Follow-Up Suggestions

Use the ornaments created by the students to create a mobile titled, "Sometimes I Like Being Alone."

Reinforce the idea of being happiest alone during certain activities, such as independent reading.

Sensitivity Issues

While this activity promotes the idea of being content with our own company, it should be recognized that this applies in certain situations only and that having friends and interacting with others is critical to personal development and mental well-being. Students should be encouraged not to use "being happy alone" as an excuse for not joining in shared activities.

Activity Links

Things That Make Me Happy ....pp. 54–55
Can I Play? ....pp. 94–95

Answers

Teacher check

Finally, some time to myself!

Being alone doesn't mean you have to feel lonely. In fact, being on your own can feel really good.

1. Billy likes to read by herself. Think of some other things that are fun or relaxing to do on your own. Write some of them on Billy's book.

What is your favorite thing to do on your own?

2. (a) Draw yourself on the circle on the left doing your favorite "alone" thing. Complete the sentence on the circle on the right.

(b) Cut around the circles and glue them back to back.

(c) Punch a hole in the top, attach string and hang to display.

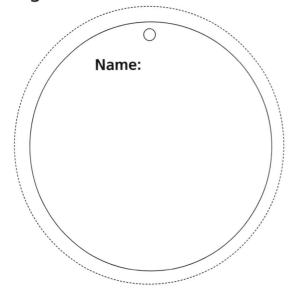

Name:

When I am alone, I like to ...

_____

_____

Dealing With Exclusion

Indicators

- Understands people make choices about whom they play with.
- Accepts decisions made by others.
- Identifies reasons why someone may choose not to play with him/her.

Pre-Lesson Focus Discussion

Invite the students to share experiences when they have not been able to play with their person of choice. Investigate why their friend chose not to play with them on that occasion. Discuss whether it was fair to be left out and how it made them feel.

Encourage the students to think of what they could do in a situation where they cannot play with their person of choice. Determine whether each solution is a positive or negative way to deal with the problem and whether the solution will help them to be included in the future.

Using the Student Activity Sheet

1. Look at the cartoon at the top of the student activity page. Have the students suggest reasons why Della might not want to play with Billy today. Discuss how Billy feels and whether or not her response to Della was positive.

2. Read the text in bold print and refer to some of the stories shared by the students in the pre-lesson discussion about feeling left out.

3. Read Questions 1 and 2 as a class and allow the students to indicate their honest responses.

4. Read the text in bold print about the reasons people have for not playing with someone. Brainstorm to list reasons why the students may not want to or be able to play with someone sometimes. Make special note of those that are not based on whether or not the person is liked.

5. Direct the students to the cartoon in Question 3 and have them complete the speech bubble illustrating the reason they think Della does not want to play with Billy today. Allow the students to share their reasons with the class.

6. Introduce to the students the idea of their behavior causing others to not want to play with them. Encourage the students to give personality traits they would prefer not to have to deal with. Discuss the kinds of behaviors that make them want to play with a person. To complete Question 4, ask the students to write about something they might do that could make others not want to play with them.

Follow-Up Suggestions

Create an action plan of "What to do when my friend won't play with me." The plan should include suggestions the students derive for alternative play arrangements and for addressing the issue of being left out.

Sensitivity Issues

Students will be better able to cope with exclusion when they feel they have a plan of "what to do" in such a situation. One of the most upsetting aspects of this kind of rejection is the embarrassment of having no alternative and being left aimless. Equipping students with possible alternatives to occupy themselves in these situations will ease any embarrassment or loneliness the student may be experiencing, while diffusing problems which are the cause of or may result from the situation.

Activity Links

Answers

Teacher check

**Have you ever felt left out?
Sometimes the friends we want to play
with don't want to play with us!**

1. Do you have friends? | **yes - lots** \ **yes - a few** \ **no - not really**

2. When do you feel left out? | **all the time** \ **sometimes** \ **never**

**Most of the time there is a good reason why a friend won't play with you—
and usually it is NOT because he/she doesn't like you.**

3. In the speech bubble, write a reason why Della might not want to play
   with Billy today.

4. Write about something a person could do that might make his/her
   friends not want to play with him/her.

_____

_____

_____

Exclusion: Action Plan

Indicators

- Understands that people can control their own behavior but not the behavior of others.
- Makes sensible suggestions for resolving disagreements with peers.
- Suggests alternative play arrangements for times when "left out."

Pre-Lesson Focus Discussion

Describe a situation familiar to the students where someone might be left out; for example, wanting to share equipment when there is not enough to go around or wanting to join a game of tag, but not being encouraged to play by friends. Have the students use body language to show how they would feel in such a situation. Ask the students to think about when they have seen someone with this kind of body language.

Using the Student Activity Sheet

1. Look at the cartoon at the top of the student activity page. Ask the students whether they have ever been in a situation where they asked questions like this. How does it feel when they don't know what to do?

2. Explain to the students that they can take charge of the situation in a number of ways. First, they can speak politely to the person who has left them out and try to find out why. Read the text in bold print at the top of the page, then Question 1. Allow the students to write what they could do to try to make up with their friend.

3. Reaffirm the idea that it is all right to be left out sometimes and that others may have very good reasons for doing so. Read the text in bold print about accepting the decisions our friends make, and direct discussion towards positive things we can do when we have been left out. Brainstorm to list possible activities.

4. Look at the pictures at the bottom of the page showing things the students can do to occupy themselves when they are left out. Have the students describe what is happening in each and match them to one of the three descriptions in Question 2.

5. Allow the students time to cut out and glue the pictures into the appropriate spaces.

Follow-Up Suggestions

Encourage the students to draw upon the three ideas suggested in Question 2 when they are in a situation where they are left out.

Provide a box of special "things to do" for students who are having a "left out" day to borrow from.

Sensitivity Issues

Students who are left out on a regular basis will, over time, become more and more despondent and less able to employ skills for making and keeping friends. These students should be closely monitored and provided with support from staff to help them re-enter friendship circles.

Activity Links

Answers

Teacher check

Did I do something wrong?

What am I going to do now?

Sometimes we upset our friends by being silly or careless. Sometimes they choose not to play with us anymore.

1. What could you do to make up with your friend?

_____

_____

If your friend still won't play with you, that's okay.

Remember that you can't MAKE your friends play with you. Everyone has days when they are left on their own. Here are some ideas to help you find something to do on your "left out" days.

2. Cut out the pictures and glue them onto the matching spaces.

Look for other people to play with.	Keep busy. Go to the library or play with a ball.	Offer to help someone out.

Stranger Danger

Indicators

- Understands that every adult is not a friend.
- Understands that some adults use tricks and tell lies to make children do things they shouldn't.
- Is prepared to say "no" to an adult in order to protect himself/herself.

Pre-Lesson Focus Discussion

Read or tell the story of "Little Red Riding Hood" to the students. Discuss the tricks that the Big Bad Wolf used to try to get Little Red Riding Hood to do things she was not allowed to do. Discuss how Little Red Riding Hood dealt with the wolf. Allow the students to suggest other things Little Red Riding Hood could have done to protect herself.

Encourage the students to share stories about real-life "big bad wolves" they have heard about and invite them to share what they would do if confronted with such a person.

Using the Student Activity Sheet

1. Look at the cartoon at the top of the student activity page and ask the students what the man is trying to do. Discuss what would be the best thing for Billy to do in this situation.
2. Discuss what "bad" adults look like. Explain to the students that "bad" people look like any other people. They are often well-dressed and well-spoken and very clever at pretending to be someone that a child could trust. Have the students explain who a "stranger" is; in other words, anyone they do not know. Read the text to reiterate what has been discussed and stress the importance of saying "no" to strangers and continuing to say "no" until they are safely away.
3. Direct the students to the three "stranger" speech bubbles. Read each of the scenarios and have the students say "no" together as a class in response to what Billy should say in each case.
4. Allow the students time to trace and color each "no" response to complete the activity.

Follow-Up Suggestions

Role-play a wide variety of situations when a stranger uses a trick or tells a lie to get a child to do something unsafe. Have the students respond with a resounding "no." Continually challenge students to decide what is "safe" and what is "not safe" to do with a stranger.

Encourage the students to be on the lookout for strangers hanging around the school and to see a staff member if they have any concerns.

Sensitivity Issues

Though it is easy to make excuses for why an apparent stranger may be in or around a school, it is better not to take risks, and all unidentified people should be confronted by a staff member to confirm their identity. Schools should also issue "visitor" badges for all non-staff visiting the school. Many schools also have policies concerning any adults, parents, or relatives with restraining orders who pose a threat to students in the school. Such policies should be followed closely.

Activity Links

Answers

Teacher check

Hi, Billy. Your mom told me to give you a lift home.

But ... I don't know you!

It is great to be friendly. But you need to be careful—not everyone is a friend! Some strangers are bad people and tell lies to make you think they are a friend. When a stranger asks you to do something—say "NO!"

Look at each bubble on the right. Trace and color the letters to show what Billy should say to these strangers.

Hop in. Your mom told me to give you a lift. Hurry!

NO!

Come here, Billy! I've got a puppy. Do you want to carry him to my house for me?

NO!

NO!

Here, Billy, have a chocolate bar. I've got more in my car. Come with me and you can have them.

Being Positive Around Others

Indicators

- Understands that being positive makes people more appealing to be around.
- Identifies the types of attitude he/she displays around others.

Pre-Lesson Focus Discussion

Use puppets to create a very positive character and a very negative character. Encourage the students to suggest the types of things each character might say and to choose which character they would prefer to have as a friend. Have the students give reasons to explain their choice of friend.

Using the Student Activity Sheet

1. Look at the cartoon at the top of the student activity page and decide with the class whether Billy has a positive or a negative attitude.

2. Read the text in bold print and experiment with the way people can say different things to make them sound positive or negative. Encourage the students to say things such as "Hi" or "Let's go" in a positive or a negative way.

3. Direct the students to the cartoons in Question 1. Read each one with the students and then ask them to color the cartoons that best describe the way they talk and behave around others.

4. Read Question 2 (a) and (b). Instruct the students to color either the check or the cross under each of the cartoons to indicate whether they would like to be friends with someone who talks or behaves in that way.

5. Challenge the students to think about whether the way they talk and behave helps them to make and keep friends or not.

Follow-Up Suggestions

Discuss what the students could do to help someone who is talking or behaving in a negative way to encourage them to be happier and more positive.

Use music to demonstrate how the students' moods can change when they are exposed to different situations. Have them change their body movements and their facial expressions to represent the mood of the music.

Sensitivity Issues

Emphasize to the students that they can control their behavior and can choose to be positive or negative in their outlook in order to cope with situations that confront them. However, it is still important to acknowledge how they really feel, as this will assist them to work through problems and seek help if they need it.

Activity Links

What I'm Like On the Inside ....pp. 8–9

Things I'm Good At ....pp. 10–11

Let's Celebrate! ....pp. 20–21

Being My Best...pp. 24–25

What I Think of Me.......................................pp. 40–41

How Do You Feel? ....pp. 48–49

Encouraging Others to Try ....pp. 74–73

Grumpy Grouch..pp. 92–93

Are You Okay?...pp. 108–109

Answers

Teacher check

The things we say and the way we say them can help us to make friends.

1. Look at the cartoons below. Color those that remind you of the way you talk and behave.

2. (a) Color the checks under the boxes showing someone you would like to have as a friend.

(b) Color the crosses under the boxes showing someone you would not like to have as a friend.

Influencing Others Positively

Indicators

- Understands what is meant by the term "encourage."
- Suggests ways people can encourage others.
- Provides encouragement for a peer.

Pre-Lesson Focus Discussion

Say encouraging things to a number of different students in the class. Ask how it made them feel to be encouraged and what it made them feel like doing.

Play circle games where the students are required to say something encouraging to one another. For example, take turns going around the circle to say something encouraging to the person alongside.

Using the Student Activity Sheet

1. Look at the cartoon at the top of the student activity page and discuss how Della was feeling about her efforts. Evaluate whether or not Sam's comment is encouraging, and suggest other ways he could have responded that may or may not have been encouraging.

2. Read the text in bold print describing what "encouragement" is. Have the students attempt to explain in their own words what they think encouragement means.

3. Read Question 1 and ensure the students are clear about how to create their secret message.

4. Allow the students time to write their message, cut it out and fold it in half. When complete, the students can "secretly" pass their encouraging message to the appropriate person.

Follow-Up Suggestions

Create a special bulletin board for the "Star of the Week." Randomly choose a different student every week to create a display of photos, comments and achievements to encourage that person.

Have the students write encouragement awards for one another to hand out at a special class awards ceremony.

Sensitivity Issues

While teachers should ensure that every student in their class is given encouragement, it is important that all comments are sincere, as even very young students are extremely perceptive. Empty encouragement is of little value and will undermine future efforts to offer genuine encouragement to a student.

Activity Links

Answers

Teacher check

You can help your friends to try their hardest by telling them what you like about them. Maybe you like something they do or how they act. This is called "encouragement."

1. Send a secret message to encourage one of your friends.

    (a) Cut out the secret message envelope below.

    (b) Write an encouraging message to your friend.

    (c) Fold and decorate the message and give it to your friend.

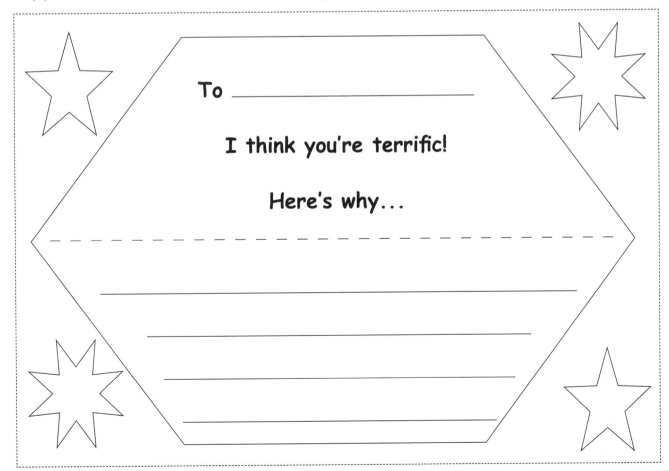

To _____

I think you're terrific!

Here's why...

Caring About the Feelings of Others

Indicators

- Understands that others have feelings that can be hurt.
- Identifies different ways people can demonstrate that they care about others.

Pre-Lesson Focus Discussion

Discuss the types of things the students do for and say to their friends. Encourage the students to share stories about times they have done something extra special for a friend. Discuss how the gesture made them and their friend feel.

Hypothesize about what the world would be like if everyone genuinely cared about the feelings of others.

Using the Student Activity Sheet

1. Look at the cartoon at the top of the student activity page. Discuss how sharing could make their friends feel. Is sharing a caring thing to do?

2. Discuss the text in bold print and ask the students to make suggestions as to how they could show their friends they care about them.

3. Direct the students to Question 1 and have them write the names of five friends on the strips as described.

4. Read the "Five great ways to show you care" written in the boxes at the bottom of the page. Discuss them and encourage the students to give examples for some of the suggestions. Have the students cut out the boxes and choose a friend to glue each of the suggestions next to. The students should think carefully about the friends they choose and what each would best appreciate.

5. Allow the students to cut out the completed strips and loop them together to complete their friendship chain.

Follow-Up Suggestions

Join the strips into a class chain using contributions from all of the students in the class. Join the ends to complete a "circle of friends" for display.

Encourage the students to demonstrate their friendship by using the links of their chain to remind them of how they can care for the individual friends they chose.

Sensitivity Issues

Students should feel free to choose their favorite five friends for this activity, as the point is not to make sure everyone is being cared for, but rather to develop an understanding of *how* to be caring. Maintain the perspective of "who I can care for" rather than "who cares for me." Avoid drawing attention to whom each person chose. Instead, focus on the fact that we all have friends and special people we like to care for.

Activity Links

Answers

Teacher check

I love to share with my friends.

There are many ways to show you care about your friends. Can you think of some?

1. (a) Think of five friends you have. Write their names on the lines on the paper strips below.

(b) Five great ways to show you care about someone are written in the boxes opposite. Cut out each one and glue it onto a name band above to show how you could care about that friend.

(c) Cut out the name strips and glue them into a paper chain.

I can tell you I like you.

I can give you a hug.

I can play with you.

I can give you a present.

I can help you.

Caring About the Safety of Others

Indicators

- Identifies unsafe behaviors.
- Understands that friends care about each other's safety.
- Suggests what he/she could do to try to keep others safe.

Pre-Lesson Focus Discussion

Encourage the students to share stories about times when they have seen others doing dangerous things. Talk about what happened or what could have happened and also what they did or could have done to demonstrate that they cared about the safety of others.

Review safe and unsafe areas around the school, and identify the risks in unsafe locations.

Using the Student Activity Sheet

1. Look at the cartoon at the top of the student activity page. Discuss what is happening in the cartoon and have the students predict what might happen next.

2. Discuss whether or not the students would allow their friends to do dangerous things, and have them give reasons for their answers. The students can then use the information from this discussion to complete Question 1.

3. Direct the students to the cartoon at the bottom of the page. Discuss what is happening in the picture. Encourage the students to identify safe and unsafe activities in the playground. Instruct the students to circle the unsafe activities to complete Question 2.

4. Invite the students to share experiences they may have had or witnessed where others on the playground were doing some of the unsafe activities in the cartoon. To complete Question 3, discuss what a good friend would do if they saw someone do any of these things .

Follow-Up Suggestions

Go for a walk around the school grounds, pausing in a number of different locations. In each location, discuss the safe and unsafe activities students might participate in.

Have the students write short recounts of something unsafe they have witnessed or been part of in their school grounds. Conclude the stories with "If only I had" as a reminder message as to how we can handle such situations in the future. Display the stories with the heading "If only ... "

Sensitivity Issues

Students should be made aware they can only advise other students to behave in a safe manner—they can not control them or make them do something they are unwilling to do. Advise the students that the best way to keep their friends safe is to only be involved in safe activities themselves and to set an example for others.

Activity Links

Answers

1. Answers will vary
2. Kid about to touch unknown object (syringe), kid chasing ball onto the road, kid standing on roof of play equipment.

   Note: Some students may consider the kid on top of the monkey bars is unsafe.
3. Teacher check

Good friends don't let friends do dangerous things.

1. Would you stop a friend who was going to do something dangerous?

   | Yes | No |

   Why? _____

   _____

2. Which of these little goats are doing things that are not safe in the picture below? Find and circle them.

3. Discuss what a good friend would do if they saw someone do any of these dangerous things.

Using Good Manners

Indicators

- Understands the purpose of using manners.
- Understands when and how to use manners.
- Demonstrates manners in everyday situations.

Pre-Lesson Focus Discussion

Teach the students words for "please" and "thank you" in a number of different languages. Explain that people all over the world use manners. Invite the students to suggest reasons why manners might be used worldwide.

Brainstorm to list things we say to one another which demonstrate good manners.

Using the Student Activity Sheet

1. Look at the cartoon at the top of the student activity page. Discuss the idea of saying "please" when you need help with something.

2. Read the text in bold print about how manners make other people feel. Discuss why using manners might make someone feel special or important. Review all the ways manners are used in the classroom to keep it a friendly, happy place. Imagine what the classroom might be like if no one used good manners. How would the teacher behave? How would the students behave? Would it be a fun, safe place to be?

3. Ask the students whether they use good manners in the classroom and have them indicate their response to complete Question 1.

4. Direct the students to the "Manners Die" template. Read the instructions on how it is to be assembled. Take time to demonstrate the construction of a cube, then allow the students to construct their own. Note: This activity will be most successful when copied onto light card stock.

5. Give the students time with a peer to use their die as a guide for role-playing some situations where manners are used. For example, if the child rolls a "Please," he/she needs to think of a situation where the word "please" is needed and role-play it with a partner.

Follow-Up Suggestions

Be diligent about enforcing the use of manners in class. Praise students for remembering to use manners, describing how it made you feel to hear them.

Sensitivity Issues

Refrain from using disciplinary measures to enforce the use of manners. Manners are best taught through example and appreciation of effort.

Activity Links

Answers

Teacher check

When we use good manners, we make other people feel special and important. We use different manners at different times.

In class, we show good manners when we sit still, look at and listen to the teacher.

Sam, would you please help me clean up?

Of course.

1. Do you use good manners in the classroom?

Yes	No

2. Make a cube by folding and gluing the template together to create a "Manners Die."

3. Take turns rolling the die with a friend and pretend you are doing something where you need to use the manners shown on the die.

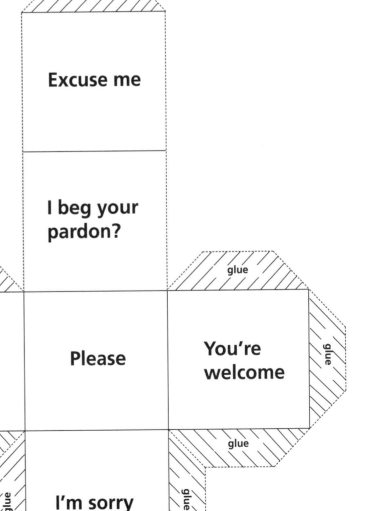

glue

Excuse me

I beg your pardon?

glue   glue

glue

Thank you   **Please**   **You're welcome**   glue

glue   glue

glue   **I'm sorry**   glue

Trying Hard At School

Indicators

- Understands the benefits of trying hard.
- Appreciates that the effort people put into activities affects how much they enjoy them and how they feel about themselves.
- Predicts how effort may affect a person's future success and ability to make friends.

Pre-Lesson Focus Discussion

Encourage the students to talk about the activities at school they really enjoy. Ask them whether they try hard at these activities and why they try hard.

Have the students imagine what it would be like not to try hard at anything. Act out a scenario pretending to not care about anything or try hard at anything. Discuss whether the person you were pretending to be would be fun to be around. What would a person like that be good at? What would be good about that person? Who would want to be friends with him/her?

Using the Student Activity Sheet

1. Draw attention to students who are sitting nicely and trying hard to listen and be cooperative. Suggest that these students (along with the remainder of the class who will now be doing their best to show effort also) must be learning a lot and getting better at things every day because they try so hard.

2. Look at the cartoon at the top of the student activity page. Have the students comment upon the amount of effort Billy is putting in.

3. Read the text in bold print about people who try hard. Ensure the students understand that they should try hard at all sorts of things and in all sorts of different situations—not just at school or in the classroom.

4. Direct the students to the two children's heads and read the text for each. Have the students answer Question 1 (a) by drawing faces that show how the children might feel about themselves.

5. Discuss what life might be like for each of the children in Question 1 (a). How would they behave? What would they do or look forward to? Would they have friends? Encourage the students to write a sentence to describe what they think might happen to each of the children. Do not put a time frame on the prediction and encourage the students to write any suggestions they may have, whether short-term or long-term.

6. Invite the students to reflect upon their own effort and to predict what may happen to them in the future. Allow them to document their thoughts to complete Questions 2 and 3.

Follow-Up Suggestions

Reward students' efforts with encouragement awards.

Provide the students with a framework for goal-setting and encourage them to work towards achieving a special goal or developing a particular skill in the future.

Sensitivity Issues

Students who appear not to be trying at school may be experiencing difficulties emotionally or physically. Be careful to encourage students in a way that sets achievable goals that can be easily rewarding for tentative students. Do not make an example of students who appear not to be trying, to avoid compounding existing issues.

Activity Links

Answers

Teacher check

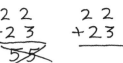

People who try hard become good at lots of things. They learn faster and have more fun!

1. Look at the children in these two pictures.

   (a) Draw faces to show how you think the children feel about themselves.

I try hard.

I don't try.

   (b) Write a sentence to describe what you think might happen to each of these children.

   _____   _____

   _____   _____

   _____   _____

   _____

2. Are you a person who tries hard at school? Yes \ No

3. What do you think might happen to you?

   _____

   _____

Forgiving Others

Indicators

- Acknowledges that people are not perfect and will make mistakes.
- Understands the importance of saying "sorry" in order to resolve conflict.
- Understands the importance of accepting an apology and forgiving others in order to resolve conflict.

Pre-Lesson Focus Discussion

Write the word "sorry" for the students to see. Have them attempt to explain what sorry means in their own words. Brainstorm to list some situations where they might need to say sorry. Draw or write the situations around the word "sorry."

Ask the students what happens when someone says sorry to them. What should they do? What should they say? What has to happen so the two people can be friends again?

Using the Student Activity Sheet

1. Look at the cartoon at the top of the student activity page. Discuss what is happening and the outcome of the scenario. Make a special point of noting that both people have a responsibility to work the problem out–not just the person who made the mistake.

2. Read the text in bold print about forgiving others and how it makes us and the person we are forgiving feel. Encourage the students to attempt to put "forgiveness" into their own words.

3. Read the cloze sentences in Question 1. Assist the students as a whole class to select the correct word from the box to complete each sentence in the story. Allow the students time to write the correct words.

4. Look at the faces template and read through the instructions in Question 2. Demonstrate how to construct the back-to-back faces and allow the students time to color and complete the activity independently.

Follow-Up Suggestions

Draw attention to scenarios in books or those which come up in the playground or classroom between students which need to be resolved. Encourage the students to suggest how the problem could be resolved and the people involved could become friends again. Emphasize the importance of saying "I'm sorry" and "I forgive you."

Role-play simple scenarios using puppets where a problem is resolved by saying "I'm sorry" and "I forgive you."

Discuss the different ways we could say "sorry" and note the difference in tone when a person really means it.

Sensitivity Issues

Saying "sorry" is often not easy to do, particularly when someone is angry, hurt, or upset. Similarly, being able to forgive someone will become increasingly more difficult to do when people have to deal with some kind of loss or emotional pain. While many school-based scenarios can be dealt with relatively easily by encouraging the students to be genuine in saying "sorry" and offering forgiveness, more serious cases may require considerable time for the subjects to cool down, discuss what has happened, and consider a range of solutions before ultimately resolving the issue.

Activity Links

Answers

1. unhappy, sorry, forgive, happy
2. Teacher check

Everyone does the wrong thing sometimes. When we forgive others, it makes us feel better about ourselves for being a good person and helps the person who hurt us feel okay again.

1. Use the words in the box to complete this story about forgiving others.

unhappy	happy	sorry	forgive

Billy did something wrong. She felt so _____.

She told Sam she was _____.

Sam said, "I _____ you."

Now Billy feels _____ again.

2. Color and cut out the circles. Fold in half at the fold line. Attach a string and hang to display, or form a loop with elastic and wear it around your wrist.

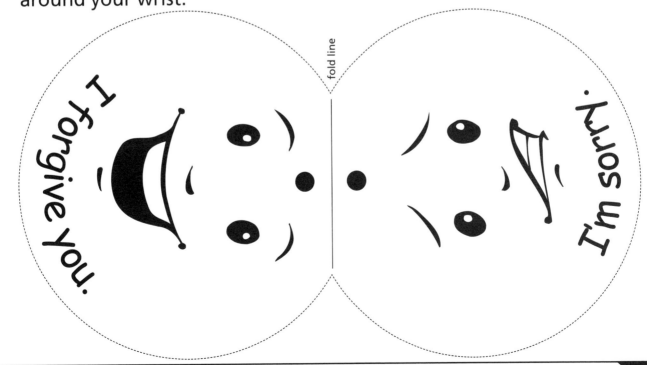

Acceptance of Others

Indicators

- Understands that people are all unique.
- Recognizes that people differ in their looks, behavior and beliefs.
- Demonstrates acceptance of others despite their differences.

Pre-Lesson Focus Discussion

Provide stimulus pictures of a number of different looking people wearing an assortment of clothes and doing a variety of things. Have the students suggest ways in which they are different from the people in the pictures.

Draw attention to the ways in which the people in the pictures are similar to one another, and discuss whether or not the students in the class also share these similarities. Make special note of the way people feel. Would the people in the pictures experience the same feelings as students in the class?

Using the Student Activity Sheet

1. Look at the cartoon at the top of the student activity page, with Billy showing concern about the way she has been behaving. Discuss why Della may have responded the way she did. Question the students about people they are still friends with in spite of them behaving differently.

2. Read the text in bold print about what makes people different. Share something you have learned as a result of being friends with someone different from yourself. Encourage the students to share something they have learned as a result of being friends with someone different from them.

3. Direct the students to the picture of Taj, the alien from Planet Zog. Have the students color him, using the colors suggested in Question 1.

4. Discuss the way Taj looks and allow the students to list a number of ways Taj is different from them to complete Question 2.

5. Ask the students what they think Taj would be like. Would he be friendly? How could they find out? Read Question 3 and have the students decide whether or not they could be friends with someone like Taj. Allow the students to share the reasons behind their answer.

6. Suggest to the students that they are required to make friends. Brainstorm to list the kinds of things they might do to strike up a friendship with someone as different as Taj. What would they say? How would they act? How might he feel in response to their efforts to make friends with him? Allow the students to choose their favorite ideas for making friends with Taj and write them in answer to Question 4.

Follow-Up Suggestions

Relate the suggested means of making friends with different people to establishing new friendships in the class. Encourage the students to make friends with someone they do not usually spend time with and to choose someone who is quite different from them.

Write a wall story about meeting different kinds of people in the community or in a "round the world" adventure, including some of the fascinating things they can teach us.

Sensitivity Issues

Refrain from using students in the class as an example of what's "different," particularly differences relating to race, faith, or disabilities. For class-based discussions, focus on creating a sense of "belonging to the class" or the same community to demonstrate sameness. Ensure the students are aware of the feelings all people share about being accepted or left out as a means of promoting equal acceptance of all students.

Activity Links

Answers

Teacher check

There are many different kinds of people. People look different, behave in different ways and believe different things. Making friends with different kinds of people is a great way to find out new things and lead an interesting life.

1. This is Taj, from the Planet Zog. Color him using only red, purple and green pencils.

2. How is Taj different from you?

_____

_____

_____

_____

_____

3. Could you be friends with Taj?
   Yes \ **No**

4. What would you do to make friends with Taj?

_____

_____

_____

_____

_____

Encouraging Others to Join In

Indicators

- Recognizes behaviors which encourage others to join in and feel accepted.
- Cooperates when playing a board game.
- Demonstrates a willingness to join in and to encourage others to play with him/her.

Pre-Lesson Focus Discussion

Encourage the students to share experiences where they have not felt like they could join in and play with a group. How did they feel? What did they do? Was there a good reason why they couldn't join in on that occasion?

Have the students imagine they are playing in a game with a group of friends and they see a person who wants to join in. What should they do? Make up other imaginary people who are "different" in some way and ask whether or not they should be encouraged to join in.

Using the Student Activity Sheet

1. Direct the students to the board game on the student activity page. Read the instructions as a class and review the basic rules for fair play.

2. Provide the students with counters and dice. Either divide the class into small groups of no more than four or allow the students to establish their own small groups by inviting one another to join in their game.

3. Allow the students time to play the game, reading about the different scenarios students may come across in the playground as they move across the board.

4. Have the students come back together as a whole class to recall some of the things written in the boxes and whether or not there were penalties or rewards associated with them. Encourage the students to assess whether or not these penalties and rewards were fair.

Follow-Up Suggestions

Provide a large plastic bin full of sporting equipment and games at recess for the students to use as "game starters" with their peers. Encourage the students to invite new people to join their games.

Brainstorm to list games the students could play without a teacher's guidance during recess. Review the way they would need to behave as part of a large group in order for the game to work. Discuss what would happen if the players did not cooperate.

Sensitivity Issues

When forming groups to play the board game, ensure all students are accounted for and made to feel like valued group members. It may help to discuss what it feels like to be left out prior to forming groups, and to remind students to include those who are shy or find it difficult to interact with peers. Similarly, students should also be reminded that if asked to join a group, it is good manners to accept the invitation despite what their personal preferences may be.

Activity Links

Answers

Teacher check

START

Ask a friend to play this game with you. Take turns using a die and counters to move along the path. Read what it says in the boxes when you land on them and follow the instructions.

You tell a friend he/she can't play with you. **Go back 2 spaces.**

You ask the new kid to play with you. **Go ahead 4 spaces.**

You leave out someone and hurt his or her feelings. **Go back 3 spaces.**

You start a game of soccer. **Go ahead 3 spaces.**

You ask if you can join a jump rope game. **Go ahead 4 spaces.**

You are mean to someone. **Go back 4 spaces.**

You're a winner!

Being Attentive

Indicators

- Understands that listening to others is polite.
- Understands that listening to others lets them know you are interested in them.
- Demonstrates attentive listening skills

Pre-Lesson Focus Discussion

Ask the students about their day and role-play poor listening skills to them by pretending not to listen to what they are saying. Ask the students to share how it made them feel when they weren't really being heard.

Have the students suggest how we could let someone know that we are really listening to them. Encourage the students to role-play what good listening skills look like.

Using the Student Activity Sheet

1. Look at the cartoon at the top of the student activity page. Ask the students if they have ever felt like someone was not really listening to them. Discuss the difference between "hearing" someone talking to you and "listening" to what he/she is saying.

2. Read the text in bold print explaining how not listening to a person can make him/her feel. Review behaviors which are polite and demonstrate good manners. Have the students turn to the person next to them and practice using good listening skills while they take turns to tell each other about a given topic, such as what they had for lunch.

3. To complete Question 1, refer back to the cartoon and have the students decide whether or not Billy was being a good listener.

4. Have the students deduce from Billy's listening skills whether or not she was being a good friend and indicate their response to complete Question 2.

5. Direct the students to the unfinished cartoon in Question 3. Have the students draw what they think Billy should have been doing and saying when Della was talking to her. They can then write a short sentence describing what they have drawn to complete Question 3 (b).

Follow-Up Suggestions

Establish cues for the students to stop, look and listen to the teacher and encourage the use of effective listening skills in the classroom; for example, three claps may represent "mouths closed," "arms folded" and "eyes on the teacher."

Sensitivity Issues

Being a role model for acceptable listening skills is crucial for teachers. Take time to listen to students politely and to expect the same in return. Students should be encouraged to understand that even if they are shy or find it difficult to interact with others, it is not all right for them to be inattentive. Everyone has a responsibility to the person who is talking to listen and respond appropriately.

Activity Links

Good Manners ....pp. 80–81
Grumpy Grouch...pp. 92–93

Answers

Teacher check

Have you ever had the feeling that the person you are talking to is not listening? It can make you feel upset! It is good manners to listen when someone is speaking to you. Listening and being interested is one way to let your friends know you care about them.

1. Do you think Billy is being a good listener? **Yes** \ **No**

2. Do you think Billy is being a good friend? **Yes** \ **No**

3. (a) Draw Billy in this picture, showing what you think she should be doing.

(b) What is Billy doing in your picture?

_____

_____

Being Positive and Happy

Indicators

- Understands that a person's mood affects the way other people feel about him/her.
- Recognizes unfavorable personality traits.

Pre-Lesson Focus Discussion

Draw a large "smile" shape on a sheet of paper for the students to see. Discuss how seeing a happy person makes us feel. What do they think of happy people? What do they want to do when they are around happy people? How do they feel when they are around happy people?

Turn the paper upside down so that the "smile" shape becomes a frown. Have the students show a frown on their own face and ask the same questions again in reference to unhappy people. What do they think of unhappy people? What do they want to do when they are around unhappy people? How do they feel when they are around unhappy people?

Ask the students to share their preference. Lead them to decide to turn the paper back around to the "happy" shape.

Using the Student Activity Sheet

1. Look at the cartoon at the top of the student activity page. Discuss what is happening in the cartoon and why Sam might be behaving the way he is. Consider how his response to Della's invitation would have made Della feel.
2. Read the text in bold print and direct the students to the picture of the "grumpy grouch" to which it refers. Ask the students whether it would be fun to play with someone who is being a grumpy grouch like the character drawn. Allow the students to color the grumpy grouch.
3. Read the words down the side of the page with the students. Have them decide which words describe a grumpy person and underline them.
4. Allow the students time to copy the words they underlined into the grumpy grouch's picture to complete Question 2.
5. Encourage the students to reflect upon how they behave and describe their mood using some of the words in Question 2 to complete Question 3.

Follow-Up Suggestions

Make a fun, friendly person as a whole class by drawing and cutting out a giant shape with a big smile and allowing the students to color it in bright, "happy" colors. Brainstorm to list words that describe people who are positive and happy and write them onto flashcards. The students can them attach these positive words to the picture of the giant.

Sensitivity Issues

It is important not to be dismissive of the emotions being displayed by students who are feeling bad. This activity is designed to educate students about their potential to have an impact on other students and how this can affect their ability to make friends. It should not be used to reduce the seriousness of any emotional difficulties a student may be experiencing.

Activity Links

Answers

Teacher check

There is nothing worse than a grumpy grouch! No one likes being around frowning people. That's not fun at all!

1. Color the grumpy grouch.

2. Read the words down the side of the page. Copy the words that describe a grumpy grouch into his picture.

friendly

mean

kind

sad

angry

fun

rude

happy

3. Tell how you behave around your friends.

_____

_____

Joining In

Indicators

- Understands that he/she can politely ask to join in with others.
- Understands that he/she may not always be able to join in with the people he/she chooses.
- Demonstrates a willingness to join in with others.

Pre-Lesson Focus Discussion

Invite the students to form a circle and ask three of them to pretend they are playing a game with an imaginary ball inside the circle. Encourage the students surrounding them to pretend (one at a time) that they would like to join the game, and demonstrate how they would go about joining in.

Discuss the different strategies used by the students to join in with the others. Consider which were the most effective, which were not so effective, and why.

Using the Student Activity Sheet

1. Look at the cartoon at the top of the student activity page. Ask the students whether they have ever wanted to join in a game but were too frightened to ask. Discuss whether or not they were happy they did not ask or if they wished they had.

2. Read the text in bold print about asking to join in a game. Discuss what is meant by the saying "If you don't ask you'll never know." Have the students suggest the kinds of things they could do if they were unable to join in. Encourage the students to take an accepting attitude towards being unable to join, but to always try again another day.

3. Direct the students to the finger puppets of the little goats. Demonstrate how the finger puppets are constructed and allow the students time to color, cut out and construct their own puppets.

4. Have the students form pairs and provide each pair with a die.

5. Read the instructions in Questions 2 and 3 with the students. Allow them time to role-play asking to join in a game, using their puppets and the pictures on the game card.

6. When finished, encourage the students to reflect upon the games they enjoy playing and challenge them to start their own game with a view to welcoming others who may wish to play with them.

Follow-Up Suggestions

Allow the students to use their finger puppets to role-play other situations which promote inclusiveness, cooperation skills and conflict resolution.

Create a miniature puppet theater for the students to perform their plays for one another. Use the plays as stimulus for discussion about how to make and keep friends.

Sensitivity Issues

The students will need to be prepared for the possibility they will not be able to join the group of their choice. In some situations, the student may be the reason for rejection, and such issues should be treated separately. However, in most cases, the students should be reminded not to take the rejection personally, and to accept that they cannot join for a reason.

Activity Links

Answers

Teacher check

The easiest way to join in with someone's game is to just ask! If they say "no," you can find something else to do. But if you don't ask at all, you might miss out on lots of fun!

May I play with you?

Sure! Let's find something to do!

1. Color, cut out and make the finger puppets below.

2. Roll a die and read the number. Match the number to one of the pictures below.

3. Use the puppets to pretend to ask if you can join in!

What are your favorite things to do? Start your own game. Who knows ... someone might ask if they can play with you!

Talking Positively Without Boasting

Indicators

- Understands the difference between talking positively and boasting.
- Understands that "showing off" is not impressive to others.
- Realizes that boasting can cause other people to feel inferior or hurt.

Pre-Lesson Focus Discussion

Introduce the word "boasting" to the students. Discuss its meaning and encourage the students to give examples of boasting.

Discuss what might make some people boast when they are trying to make friends. Think about whether or not boasting is an effective means of making friends and what kind of behavior would be more appropriate.

Using the Student Activity Sheet

1. Look at the cartoon at the top of the student activity page. Read what Sam thinks of Della and consider whether or not Della would have expected such a response.

2. Read the text in bold print together and look again at the reasons why some people might think they need to talk about themselves all the time when they are trying to make friends.

3. Brainstorm to list other ways people show off and allow the students to write an example to complete Question 1.

4. Read Question 2 (a) and (b), allowing the students to independently indicate their responses. Encourage the students to focus on one incidence of boasting they can recall and to draw this example in the space provided to complete Question 2 (c). Remind the students to use speech bubbles if there are people talking in the situation they are drawing.

5. Read the text in bold print discussing how the students can talk about themselves in a good way. Discuss why someone's feelings might be hurt by a person who is boasting.

6. Direct the students to Question 3 and have them color the goat speaking about herself in a positive way without boasting.

Follow-Up Suggestions

Draw and label self-portraits or write personal profiles, giving the students an opportunity to talk about themselves and their achievements in a safe, non-boastful context.

Sensitivity Issues

Part of creating a safe, happy environment in which the students can learn involves being diligent about the kinds of behavior we accept. Constant boasting can be a subtle form of bullying used by some students to make themselves appear more important than others and can be a threat to vulnerable students. While interfering with the natural hierarchy which will develop among the students is not recommended, teachers have a duty to protect all students by demonstrating no tolerance of bullying behavior.

Activity Links

Answers

1. Possible answers: misbehavior, being "smart," teasing, bossiness, telling "tales," bullying
2. Answers will vary
3. Goat saying "I'm a nice person."

Some people think that the best way to make friends is to talk all the time about all the things they are good at. This is called "boasting" or "showing off."

1. There are other ways people show off. Write one of them.

    _____

2. (a) Have you ever seen someone showing off? Yes \ No

    (b) Did it make you want to be his/her friend? Yes \ No

    (c) Draw a picture showing how the person was showing off. You might need to use speech bubbles to finish the picture.

It is okay to talk about yourself if you do not show off or hurt anyone else's feelings.

3. Color the goat who is talking about herself without showing off.

Telling "Tales" to Make Friends

Indicators

- Understands that sharing unkind stories about people is an inappropriate way to make friends.
- Recognizes that sharing unkind stories about others can hurt people's feelings.
- Understands that what we say about a person can influence how others will feel about him/her.

Pre-Lesson Focus Discussion

Discuss what is meant by "telling tales." Encourage the students to share examples of tales which could hurt someone's feelings.

Discuss why someone would want to share an unkind story about another person and how this might affect the way other people see the storyteller and the person about whom they are talking.

Using the Student Activity Sheet

1. Look at the cartoon at the top of the student activity page. Discuss how it makes Billy look and feel. Reflect upon times when the students have heard similar hurtful things being said about their peers or about themselves.

2. Read Questions 1 and 2 and allow the students to write their responses independently.

3. Read the text in bold print and have the students suggest the kinds of things that might be "safe" to share about others. Debate whether or not we should ever talk about others when they are not around. Discuss the difference between things that are private and things that everyone can know about.

4. Have the students explain in their own words what a friendly secret (a surprise) is and why it is special and not for sharing. Use the example of a surprise party that is kept secret from the person the party is for. What would happen if the surprise wasn't kept?

5. Direct the students to the "Friendly Secret Square" and read the instructions about how it should be constructed.

6. Demonstrate how to complete and construct a "Friendly Secret Square," and then allow the students to make their own.

7. Give the students time to share a surprise from their square privately with a friend. Encourage the students to remember not to share the new information they know about their friend with anyone else.

Follow-Up Suggestions

Play "Telephone" to illustrate how information can change when it is passed through many people.

Sensitivity Issues

When students are sharing experiences about "tale-telling," ensure they do not disclose private information or cause further embarrassment to a student who has been the subject of "talk." Guide the students to say "Once I knew someone who ... " rather than use the actual names of people involved.

Activity Links

Answers

Teacher check

Telling unkind stories about people is really mean.

1. (a) Has anyone ever told an unkind story about you? **Yes** \ **No**

   (b) How did it or how might it make you feel?

   _____

   _____

2. Do you think telling unkind stories about people is a good way to make friends? **Yes** \ **No**

If you are thinking of sharing a story about someone with your friends, always make sure it will not hurt anyone's feelings before you share it.

3. (a) This is a "Friendly Secret Square." Finish the friendly secret in each section.

   (b) Cut out the square and fold along the dotted fold lines.

   (c) Color each triangle flap a different color.

   (d) Ask your friends which color secret they want to know.

My favorite color is ... _____	I love ... _____ _____
When I grow up I want to ... _____ _____	My favorite number is ...

Joining In Without Taking Over

Indicators

- Gives examples of bossy behavior.
- Understands that being bossy and "taking over" are not friendly behaviors.
- Identifies behaviors which are appropriate when joining in and playing with others.

Pre-Lesson Focus Discussion

Have the students describe what is meant by being bossy. Discuss what bossy people do and what they sound like.

Have the students share experiences when someone has joined their game and taken over. Discuss how it made them feel and whether or not the behavior of the new person was fair and friendly.

Using the Student Activity Sheet

1. Look at the cartoon at the top of the student activity page and read the text in bold print about bossy people with the students.

2. Read Questions 1 and 2 and allow the students to reflect upon their experiences and personal behavior and indicate their responses independently.

3. Discuss the kinds of behaviors which are appropriate when joining a group or playing with others. Review such skills as listening, turn-taking, being positive and playing fair in order to be cooperative.

4. Direct the students to the puzzle pieces at the bottom of the page which combine to make up a picture of a little goat. Read through the instructions in Question 3, ensuring the students know that some of the pieces represent "bossy" behaviors and will not fit into the puzzle.

5. Allow the students time to color, cut and glue their pieces onto a separate sheet of paper.

Follow-Up Suggestions

Have the students draw outlines of themselves on a sheet of paper and write on the body parts all the friendly things they do to cooperate with others when they are playing in a group. Display the students' named pictures together with the title "We Cooperate."

Sensitivity Issues

Ensure the students do not use the names of students when sharing negative stories about bossiness and taking over. Avoid labeling students as "bossy." When a student believes he/she is seen in a certain way, he/she can come to think that kind of behavior is expected and will behave accordingly. Always separate a behavior from the person; for example, "This is Alice, who is behaving in a bossy way" rather than "Alice is bossy."

Activity Links

Answers

Teacher check

I don't like it when my friends tell me what to do all the time.

Have you ever met a bossy person? Bossy people tell everyone what to do and take over!

1. Do you think bossy people make good friends?

   Yes \ No

2. Do you tell other people what to do?

   Yes \ No

This goat is a good friend. He is not bossy.

3. (a) Color in the body parts that show the things good friends do.

   (b) Cut out the pieces you colored and glue them together on a separate sheet of paper to make a picture of your own little goat.

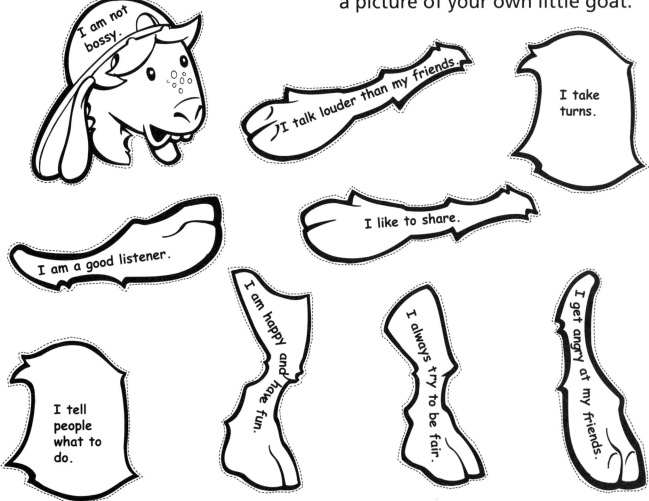

I am not bossy.

I talk louder than my friends.

I take turns.

I am a good listener.

I like to share.

I tell people what to do.

I am happy and have fun.

I always try to be fair.

I get angry at my friends.

Respecting Others

Indicators

- Understands that other people have feelings and that our actions can influence these feelings.

Pre-Lesson Focus Discussion

Bring a bunch of flowers to school and give them to a student who looks like he/she needs "cheering up." Ask the students why they think you made the gesture and how it might make the person who received them feel.

Challenge the students to think of other things they could do to help cheer someone up when he/she is feeling down.

Using the Student Activity Sheet

1. Look at the cartoon at the top of the student activity page and read the text in bold print about how the things the students do can influence the behavior of others. Encourage the students to share times when they have done something to change how someone else was feeling. Give an example of both positive and negative ways they can influence someone.

2. Explain that all people make mistakes from time to time and that sometimes we can hurt someone's feelings accidentally by saying or doing something thoughtless. Have the students think about what they would do if they hurt someone's feelings. Allow the students time to write a suggestion for what they would do if they hurt someone's feelings to complete Question 1.

3. Direct the students to Question 2 and have them suggest what might make someone feel sad. The students can imagine what they think might have happened to the child pictured and draw the event in the space provided.

4. Allow the students to explain what they have drawn to the class if they wish. Read Question 3 and have the students suggest what might make someone feel happy and draw what they think happened to make the child illustrated feel happy. Again, the students can share their pictures if they wish.

Follow-Up Suggestions

Hold a special celebration aimed at "cheering up" each other. Have the students suggest activities and games for the day and simple gestures which could be performed to help everyone feel happy and special.

Investigate celebrations held in the students' community. Find out why they exist and how it makes the people who participate in them feel.

Sensitivity Issues

Ensure the students understand that not all bad things are intentional and that it is acceptable to give someone a second chance and to let them apologize. Similarly, they need to be able to forgive themselves when they make a mistake and to make an effort to reestablish friendships which they have damaged. However, when bad things happen repeatedly or are of a serious nature, help must be sought to maintain their right to be safe and happy.

Activity Links

Answers

Teacher check

Our friends have feelings. We can do things to make those feelings good or bad. Good friends don't mean to hurt the feelings of other people.

1. If you hurt someone's feelings, what could you do?

_____

_____

2. Imagine a friend with hurt feelings. Draw or write what you think made him/her sad.

3. Imagine a friend with happy feelings. Draw or write what you think made him/her happy.

People Who Can Help Me Make Friends

Indicators

- Understands he/she can get help if he/she is having trouble making friends.
- Identifies people who can help him/her make friends.
- Understands that others can give him/her help to make friends but cannot make friends for him/her.

Pre-Lesson Focus Discussion

Use paper cutouts or shadow puppets to relate a story about a child who is new at a school and is having trouble making new friends. Include examples of how he/she has tried but nobody seems to want to know him/her. Encourage the students to offer suggestions to the child as to what he/she can do to try to make friends. Enact the students' suggestions but, each time, have the student left on his/her own with no one to play with.

Introduce the idea of the child going to someone to help him/her make friends. Have the students suggest the kinds of people who might be able to help the child make friends and what they might do to help. Use the puppet to enact the students' suggestions, with the child ultimately making friends at the new school.

Using the Student Activity Sheet

1. Look at the cartoon at the top of the student activity page. Have the students imagine being in a situation like Billy's and how she must be feeling, being unable to make friends after trying everything she can think of.

2. Read the text in bold print which suggests seeking help when someone cannot seem to make friends.

3. Direct the students to the list of people in Question 1 and have them underline three they think they could go to if they were in this situation. The students can then draw the people they chose in the boxes and write their names on the lines to complete Question 1.

4. Discuss as a class how someone might be able to help them make friends. Allow the students time to write how they would like to be helped in this situation to complete Question 2.

Follow-Up Suggestions

Create a buddy system for students who are new to the school. Discuss how the buddy system works with the class and encourage the students to make suggestions for the types of things they might do with a new person if they were his/her buddy; for example, introduce him/her to people he/she might like to be friends with, show him/her around the school, or keep him/her company at lunchtime until he/she makes friends.

Sensitivity Issues

The focus of this activity is to encourage students to "not give up" when they have exhausted all the friend-making strategies they know. Praise traits such as resilience and determination to make friends. Ensure the students understand that though they can get support and receive guidance for making friends from others, other people cannot maintain their friendships for them. The students themselves hold the responsibility for making their friendships successful.

Activity Links

Answers

Teacher check

Sometimes, no matter how hard we try, we just can't seem to make friends. This is when to ask for help. There is always someone who can help.

1. Choose three people from the list you could go to for help and draw each person in one of the boxes. Discuss how each person might be able to help you.

Mom	Dad	older brother	older sister
teacher	older student or "buddy"		school nurse

Someone else _____

1 _____

2 _____

3 _____

2. How would you like one of the people you chose to help you make friends?

_____

_____

_____

Controlling Anger

Indicators

- Understands that anger can make people behave inappropriately and make difficult situations worse.
- Understands that being angry is not an excuse for doing inappropriate things.

Pre-Lesson Focus Discussion

Discuss with the students what people who are angry look like and how they behave. Debate whether allowing themselves to become angry is acceptable.

Encourage the students to share experiences when they have become angry. What made them angry? Did getting angry help them to solve their problem? Did it make their situation worse?

Using the Student Activity Sheet

1. Look at the cartoon at the top of the student activity page. Discuss what is happening and whether or not Della's behavior is acceptable.

2. Read the text in bold print about "losing their cool." Discuss what is meant by the phrase "losing your cool" and what it means to be "cool."

3. Have the students reflect upon a time when they were angry and then complete Questions 1 and 2.

4. Direct the students to the diagram with different words and phrases in the shapes. Read the word or phrase in each shape and have the students identify which ones describe things an angry person might do. Students color the appropriate shapes containing angry behaviors to complete Question 3.

5. Read the text in bold print about making problems worse. Ask the students what kinds of silly things might be referred to. Encourage them to give examples of silly things they have witnessed or done as a result of anger. Think about the impact behaving inappropriately might have on the people around them.

6. Have the students refer back to the cartoon and determine what Della's friends might think of her when she behaves that way. Allow them to write their responses to complete Question 4.

7. Encourage the students to think of how Della could have behaved that might have been more appropriate. The students can then write something "cool" she could have said to Billy in the speech bubble provided to complete Question 5.

Follow-Up Suggestions

Brainstorm to list ideas for how the students can "cool down" when they become angry. Display the list surrounded by pictures of angry-looking people drawn by the students.

Sensitivity Issues

The ability to control anger will vary from student to student depending on the anger management that has been modeled for him/her and the severity of the situations with which he/she is confronted. Students who display inappropriate responses to anger should be removed from the group to help them "cool down" in private (removing them from their audience) and to keep other students safe.

Activity Links

Answers

1–2. Answers will vary

3. Say mean things, yell, cry, kick or hit, frown

4–5. Answers will vary

Have you ever seen people lose their "cool"? Getting angry is definitely not cool!

1. Have you ever felt angry? | Yes \ No |

2. What happened to make you feel angry? _____

_____

_____

3. Read the words in the shapes below. Color red the shapes with words that describe things an angry person might do.

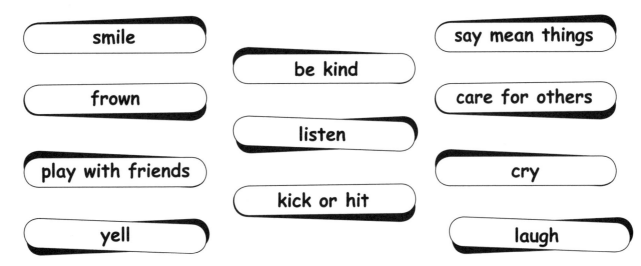

smile

be kind

say mean things

frown

care for others

listen

play with friends

cry

kick or hit

yell

laugh

Getting angry can make us do silly things and make our problems much worse. Della made her problems worse by yelling at Billy.

4. What do you think Della's friends think of her?

_____

_____

_____

5. Write something "cool" Della could have said to Billy instead of yelling at her.

Caring for Lonely People

Indicators

- Respects reasons why someone may wish to be on his/her own.
- Identifies some ways to help someone who is lonely.

Pre-Lesson Focus Discussion

Have the students sit in a circle and place a doll in the middle. Explain that the doll is feeling sad and have the students attempt to identify reasons for its sadness. Introduce the concept of loneliness. How does it feel to be lonely? How can you tell when other people are feeling lonely?

Discuss why someone might want to be on his/her own rather than playing with others. Encourage the students to think of times they just wanted to be left alone.

Using the Student Activity Sheet

1. Look at the cartoon at the top of the student activity page showing Sally sitting on her own. What is Della saying? What could Della do to make Sally feel better?

2. Read the text in bold print about reasons someone might be on his/her own. Ask the students whether they have ever felt lonely at school and have them indicate their response by answering Question 1.

3. Read the text in bold print which follows and review some of the ideas the students had in the pre-lesson discussion about helping a lonely person. Challenge the students to find and help a lonely person next time they are in the playground, but to respect that the student may wish to be left on his/her own.

4. Direct the students to the craft activity at the bottom of the page. Demonstrate how to construct the face, showing the way the strip slides to present a happy or a lonely face.

5. Read the instructions as a class about how to make it and then allow the students to construct their own to complete Question 2.

Follow-Up Suggestions

Have the students use their craft to indicate how they are feeling or to indicate how a character such as Snow White may be feeling at different stages of the story.

Have the students illustrate and write a short recount about when they feel lonely.

Sensitivity Issues

Students who experience long-term loneliness are susceptible to poor self-esteem and may require intervention to initiate and sustain friendships. While some people are happy with their own company, extended periods of isolation may lead to poor social skills and an unbalanced view of the society in which they live.

Activity Links

Answers

Teacher check

There are many reasons why someone might be on his or her own. Maybe he or she is new at school or not feeling well. Sometimes we like to be on our own. But if we are left on our own for too long, we can become lonely.

1. Do you ever feel lonely at school? **Yes** \ **No**

Helping a lonely person is easy. All you need to do is talk to the person or ask him or her to join your game.

2. (a) Cut out the face and the pull strip.

   (b) Cut slits along the dotted lines on the face.

   (c) Weave the pull strip through the slits to show a lonely or happy face.

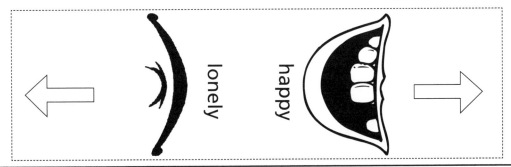

lonely

happy

Helping Others

Indicators

- Understands that being helpful fosters a positive, cooperative environment.
- Identifies ways in which people could help others.

Pre-Lesson Focus Discussion

Invite the students to do something helpful around the classroom. Give them a few minutes to carry out their helpful idea. Call them back to share what they did to be helpful. Express appreciation for all the helpful things they have done. Explain how they have made the classroom look better and saved the teacher doing extra work later on. Encourage the students to suggest how the teacher might be feeling now that he/she has less work to do. Discuss how doing something helpful for the teacher made the students feel about themselves.

Using the Student Activity Sheet

1. Look at the cartoon at the top of the student activity page and review how the teacher in the scenario might be feeling as a result of Billy being helpful.

2. Read the text in bold print about ways the students can help their friends and family as well as the teacher. Have the students suggest how they could help their friends and things they could do to be helpful at home.

3. Direct the students to the question. Read the instructions and allow the students time to complete the task independently.

Follow-Up Suggestions

Spend time "spring cleaning" the classroom as a class. Set up a range of cleaning, sorting and tidying activities for the students to help with.

Make a roster of special duties nominated students can perform; for example, cleaning the board, handing out books, collecting lunches and running errands.

Sensitivity Issues

Being helpful is something which the students need to do with a generous nature and should not be forced on them. On occasions, the students may suggest helpful things they wish to do which may not be appropriate. In these situations, encourage the students by offering them an alternative or modified task, or support a more appropriate time for the students to perform their helpful act.

Activity Links

Answers

Teacher check

There are so many ways we can help one another. We can help our friends and family and even our teacher!

Help tidy up the classroom. Draw things in the correct space on the cupboard shelves. (You can also draw containers to store them in.)

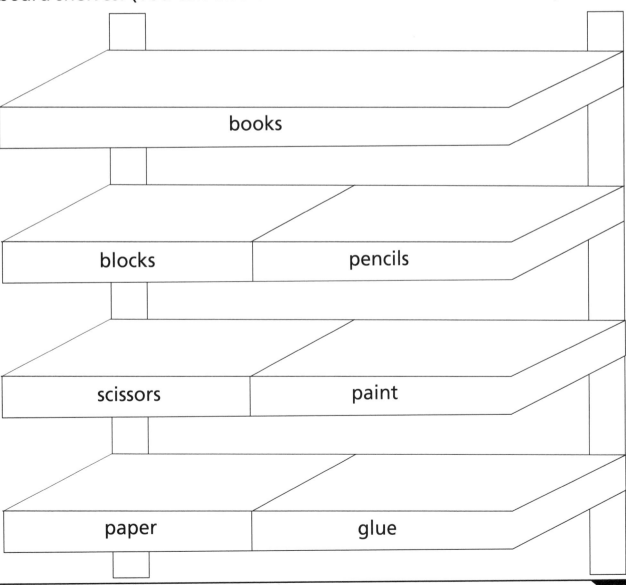

Making Good Decisions

Indicators

- Understands that people are responsible for their own behavior.

- Understands that situations will arise when people will feel pressured to do something they do not wish to do.

- Demonstrates an ability to think and make decisions independently of others.

Pre-Lesson Focus Discussion

Provide examples (either drawn, pictures, or actual objects) of items which are unsafe or inappropriate to play with. For each, provide an explanation of what it is and where it was found. Then suggest something inappropriate that you would like to do with it or encourage one of the students to do something inappropriate with it. For example, hold up a student's lunch box, explain that you found it in someone's bag and that it has yummy stuff in it. Say that you have already eaten some and try to persuade one of the students to eat something as well. Other suitable examples could include a box of matches, a bottle of paint, someone's shoes, or a packet of special marker pens.

Use the examples to place the students under pressure to make a decision contradicting what you are telling them to do and to describe how they feel being put in that position.

Using the Student Activity Sheet

1. Look at the cartoon at the top of the student activity page. Discuss what is happening and whether or not Della should participate in the trick on Billy. Ask the students how they think Della might be feeling.

2. Read the text in bold print about saying "no" when people are trying to get along and be friendly.

3. Read Question 1 and brainstorm to list the possible outcomes if Della were to agree to help. Have the students write their predictions in the space on the left-hand side of the page. Similarly, have the students suggest what the consequences may be for Della if she does not help. Allow the students time to write a suggested consequence of saying "no" in the space on the right-hand side of the page to complete Question 1.

4. Question the students as to how they would feel if they were Della and agreed to help. Would they feel comfortable with their decision? Would they be proud of themselves? Compare these feelings to how they might feel if they were able to say "no" to something they should not be doing. Have the students simplify their feelings in each situation and write their responses to complete Question 2.

5. Review the consequences of each response and how each would leave Della feeling about herself, and have the students decide what would be the best course of action for her. Ask them to imagine they are in Della's shoes. Have the students draw a picture of themselves next to the speech bubble at the bottom of the page and write what they would say to answer Question 3.

Follow-Up Suggestions

Review stranger danger and personal safety issues to ensure the students are equipped to say "no" in order to be safe.

Activity Links

Sensitivity Issues

Students with poor self-esteem who find it difficult to make and keep friends can be quite susceptible to peer pressure. When resolving these situations, the emotional status of the students involved should be considered, but cannot be used as an excuse for the student's behavior. Making excuses for poor decision-making is ultimately unsafe and will not improve the student's ability to make better decisions in the future.

Answers

Answers will vary

Getting along with people can be tricky sometimes. If your friends want you to do something that is not good, it can be hard to say "no."

1. Look at the cartoon at the top of the page. What do you think will happen if Della says...

   (a) "Yes ... I'll help"?

   _____

   _____

   _____

   (b) "No ... I won't help"?

   _____

   _____

   _____

2. How do you think Della would feel about herself if she says...

   (a) "Yes"?

   _____

   (b) "No"?

   _____

3. Draw yourself next to the speech bubble. Write what you would say in the speech bubble.

Teasing

Indicators

- Identifies how teasing makes people feel.
- Understands people can be teased or given a "hard time" by a range of others.

Pre-Lesson Focus Discussion

Discuss what is meant by the word "teasing." Encourage the students to share ways in which they have been teased and how it made them feel.

Read stories which address teasing or being "picked on." An ideal resource is the DINO-MIGHT series of three books and four posters dealing with teasing and bullying. (Didax items 2–230, 2–231, 2–232 and 2–235.)

Using the Student Activity Sheet

1. Look at the cartoon at the top of the student activity page. Discuss what Billy is saying and why she might be feeling as though everyone is "picking on her."

2. Read the text in bold print about being teased or picked on. Discuss why it could make someone want to stay home from school. What might be some of the feelings that person has? How would the students feel if they were the ones who caused someone to want to stay home from school?

3. Ask the students whether they have ever felt like they were being picked on and indicate their response to complete Question 1 (a).

4. Direct the students to the names of people in the boxes in Question 1 (b). Ask the students to color the people (or person) they felt were picking on them.

5. Refer back to the cartoon at the top of the page and brainstorm to list things Billy might be feeling in this situation. Allow the students to use the list of ideas suggested by the class to write appropriate words or phrases in the boxes provided to complete Question 2.

Follow-Up Suggestions

Have the students share experiences when they have had to be brave. Introduce the idea of having to be brave when they are being teased and reacting inappropriately to it. Make a large duck shape and have the students write something a "teaser" might say onto strips of paper to glue on its back. Give the display the title "Teasing Is Water Off a Duck's Back."

Sensitivity Issues

Teasing which happens repeatedly is harassment and should be dealt with seriously. Students who approach a teacher with concerns about being teased should be listened to and provided with adequate support and strategies to promote resilience in such situations. Teasing and bullying incidents should be recorded to identify repeat patterns among students.

Activity Links

Answers

Answers will vary

Everyone is picking on me today. It's hard to feel good about myself, but I know I'm a good person.

No one likes to be given a hard time. It can make us feel sad or angry. It might even make us feel like we don't want to go to school.

1. (a) Have you ever felt like someone was picking on you?

    Yes \ No

    (b) Who was picking on you?

    Mom or Dad   friends

    other students

    teacher   sister or brother

    no one   someone different

2. Write some words around Billy to describe how you think she feels about herself when she is given a hard time by someone.

Distinguishing Between Joking and Teasing

Indicators

- Understands that the way people talk to others affects the way they feel.
- Differentiates between joking and teasing.
- Understands the need to apologize for inappropriate comments about others.

Pre-Lesson Focus Discussion

Discuss what is meant by a "nickname." Have the students share what their nickname is (if they have one) and how they got that nickname. Ask each student if he/she likes being called by that nickname and why. Discuss why some nicknames make us feel good while others do not.

Encourage the students to share jokes they have heard. Draw attention to jokes which might be hurtful to others. Discuss why they are hurtful and whether telling such jokes is appropriate behavior.

Using the Student Activity Sheet

1. Look at the cartoon at the top of the student activity page. Discuss what is being said to Billy and whether this kind of teasing would make Billy feel good or bad.

2. Read the text in bold print about making jokes. Discuss with the students how they tell the difference between friendly and hurtful jokes.

3. Allow the students to complete Questions 1 and 2, analyzing the joke in the cartoon.

4. Direct the students to the two kinds of joking in Question 3. Encourage the students to give examples of friendly jokes and have them draw a face to show how this makes people feel. Have the students give examples of unfriendly or hurtful joking, and allow them to draw another face to indicate how that kind of joking or teasing would make someone feel.

5. Read the text in bold print about accidentally hurting someone's feelings. Explain that even if they do not intend to hurt someone's feelings or do not think what they have said is hurtful, if the person to whom it was said is made unhappy by it, they have a responsibility to apologize.

6. Have the students determine what would be appropriate to say to someone whose feelings they have hurt. Allow the students to locate and color the parts of the pattern at the bottom of the page to spell the word "sorry."

Follow-Up Suggestions

Make up a class book of friendly jokes which are not hurtful to others.

Have the students make up fun, friendly nicknames for themselves, explaining why they chose the name and why it would make them feel good if other people called them by this name.

Sensitivity Issues

The difference between joking and teasing is complex and difficult to explain to young students. Teasing of any kind should not be encouraged at this age; however, students should be encouraged to understand that playful joking is part of building solid relationships with their friends. We need to be able to keep a sense of humor in these situations and recognize when the intention of the person was to consolidate the friendship and not torment.

Activity Links

Answers

1–2. Answers will vary

3. Teacher check

4. Sorry

Everybody loves a joke. But what if the joke is about you? Some jokes are not funny to everyone. Do you know the difference?

1. Do you think this joke is funny? **Yes** \ **No**

2. Do you think Billy thinks the joke is funny? **Yes** \ **No**

There are two kinds of jokes.

3. Draw a face to show how each kind of joke makes you feel.

Friendly joking

Hurtful joking or teasing

Sometimes joking can hurt someone's feelings by accident.

4. Color the word hidden in the pattern below. Clue: It is the word we should say if we hurt someone's feelings.

	Y			R		B			B		G		G
Y				R		B		B	B		B	G	G
	Y		R		R		B			B			G
		Y		R			B		B			G	
	Y			R		B			B			G	

Y = yellow   R = red   B = blue   G= green

Dealing with Teasing

Indicators

- Identifies reasons why people tease.
- Learns a new poem about ways to deal with teasing.
- Understands that he/she has the right not to be teased and that it is the responsibility of the person teasing to stop.

Pre-Lesson Focus Discussion

Discuss what teasers and bullies are like. What do they do? How do they behave? What do other people think of them? How do people behave around them? Discuss why the students think people choose to tease others and what type of people they choose to pick on.

Using the Student Activity Sheet

1. Look at the cartoon at the top of the student activity page and discuss what Sam does in response to the teasing. Talk about whether or not this is a good strategy to use and whether the teaser got the reaction from Sam he was hoping for.

2. Read the text in bold print outlining some reasons why people tease. Allow the students to share stories about their reactions to being teased.

3. Read through the poem titled "Teasing" and invite the students to repeat each line after the teacher. Discuss the strategies introduced in the poem for how to respond to teasing. Discuss why dealing with teasing in this way could discourage a teaser. Read the final two lines and determine how the person being teased feels about himself/herself.

4. Allow the students to color the accompanying illustration and direct them to the reminder at the bottom of the page. Ensure the students understand that although it is not their fault they are being teased, there are ways to behave that discourage teasers from continuing.

Follow-Up Suggestions

Perform the poem in front of other classes to remind them of ways to deal with teasing and bullying. In between each couplet, have students act out a short scenario to describe it.

Sensitivity Issues

Students should be made aware that although the "teaser" is responsible for his/her actions and needs to learn to stop, they can minimize teasing when it occurs. Ensure that students feel secure about approaching a responsible adult who can help them deal with continued teasing and bullying, should it occur.

Activity Links

Answers

Teacher check

People tease for many reasons. They might do it to make themselves look clever or maybe to make you cry or get angry.

1. Learn the poem and find out some helpful things you can do if someone teases you.

Teasing

If you call me names,

I will not cry.

If you laugh at me,

I'll walk on by.

If you pick on me,

I will not fight.

Soon you'll find out

That I'm all right!

"I'm all right!"

Remember: It is not your fault if someone teases you.
People who tease have to learn to stop!

Keeping safe

Indicators

- Understands that all people have the right to be safe and happy.
- Determines situations that require help from an adult to resolve.
- Demonstrates a willingness to seek help in situations where he/she feels unsafe.

Pre-Lesson Focus Discussion

Discuss what is meant by "telling tales." Have the students debate whether telling tales is a good or a bad thing for students to do.

Develop a list of things they should tell a teacher about and a list of things they need to try to resolve themselves.

Using the Student Activity Sheet

1. Look at the cartoon at the top of the student activity page. Discuss what is happening and whether or not Della is in a situation she can resolve herself.

2. Read the text in bold print about bullies and how they behave to try to prevent people telling someone about what they are doing. Discuss whether or not the students believe that bullies could be "scared of being found out" and why this might be something they want to avoid.

3. Refer back to the cartoon at the top of the page and have the students write what they think Della should do in this situation to answer Question 1 (a).

4. Discuss what the girl might do if she finds out that Della has told someone about her plans to "get Sandy." Allow the students to predict and write a likely response to complete Question 1 (b).

5. Introduce the idea of seeking help from a responsible person. Discuss the kinds of people who could help them and the people who might want to help but would be unable to. Have the students determine the most reliable person to turn to in such a situation and draw his/her picture in the picture frame in Question 2. To complete the question, have the students write why that person would be the best person they could go to for help.

Follow-Up Suggestions

Review safety procedures for traveling to and from school; for example, not walking alone and sticking to public pathways where there are other people around. Identify the local "safety houses" surrounding the school and the role these houses play in the community to help keep people safe.

Sensitivity Issues

Schools will undoubtedly have a zero tolerance approach to bullying and harassment of students. Refer to your school policy documents for details of the recommended action to be taken in these situations.

Activity Links

Answers

Answers will vary

Bullies can be scary. They say things to try to stop you getting help. That is because *they* are scared of being found out.

1. Look at the cartoon at the top of the page.

    (a) What do you think Della should do?

    _____

    _____

    _____

    _____

    (b) What do you think this girl might do if she finds out Della has told someone about her?

    _____

    _____

    _____

    _____

When you tell someone you need help, make sure it is someone who really can help you.

2. Imagine you are being bullied at school.

    (a) Draw a picture of the person you would go to for help.

    (b) Write why you would go to that person for help.

    _____

    _____

    _____

    _____

Staying Away From Troublemakers

Indicators

- Understands that the people he/she spends time with can influence the types of activities he/she becomes involved in.
- Understands that spending time with troublemakers can cause him/her to get into trouble also.
- Identifies fun, safe things to do with friends.

Pre-Lesson Focus Discussion

Brainstorm to list some things that troublemakers get up to. Invite the students to think about whether they have ever been involved in any of the activities discussed or whether they have been tempted to take part. Discuss why someone might want to hang around a group of troublemakers.

Discuss what happens to troublemakers when they do silly things. Ask the students whether or not they would like that to happen to them.

Using the Student Activity Sheet

1. Look at the cartoon at the top of the student activity page showing some troublemakers. Discuss what is happening and whether or not the students think they would join them.
2. Read the text in bold print about getting into trouble. Discuss whether or not it would be a good idea to hang around people who bully and fight.
3. Read Questions 1 and 2 (a) as a class and allow the students to indicate their responses independently.
4. Brainstorm to list fun things they can do safely at school or at home without the risk of getting into trouble.
5. Allow the students to choose two ideas from the list to illustrate in the spaces provided at the bottom of the page. Have them label what they have drawn in each to complete Question 2 (b).

Follow-Up Suggestions

Compare the students' list of things troublemakers do to the list of safe, fun things they can do. Have the students determine which list looks like more fun and why.

Use the list of safe, fun things and survey the students to find out what their favorite safe, fun thing to do is. Use the data collected to construct a class graph.

Sensitivity Issues

Though troublemakers, bullies and fighters need to know they are responsible for their actions, they should be provided with opportunities to demonstrate responsible behavior. Care should be taken to encourage extended periods of responsible behavior as this will begin to mold a new identity for students who have gained a reputation for poor behavior.

Activity Links

Answers

Teacher check

There is a quick, easy way to get into trouble! Just start hanging around people who bully and fight!

1. Answer the questionnaire.

    (a) Do you get into trouble much?
    `Yes` `No`

    (b) Do you think you are a
    troublemaker? `Yes` `No`

    (c) What do you do
    with your friends?
    `Have fun` `Get into trouble`

    (d) How does it feel to get into trouble?

    _____

    _____

    _____

    _____

2. (a) Do you feel safe when you are with your friends? `Yes` `No`

    (b) Draw and label two fun, safe things you can do with friends at school.

Working Together

Indicators

- Appreciates that people can all get along together if they are friendly, caring and happy in their interactions.

Pre-Lesson Focus Discussion

Break the class into small groups of three or four students. Provide each group with construction materials such as blocks. Give the students time to work together to use all of the construction materials in their pile. Encourage them to remember to cooperate and share their ideas about how to go about the task as a team.

Using the Student Activity Sheet

1. Read the text at the top of the student activity page about getting along with others. Have the students identify the key factors in getting along; i.e., caring for themselves and caring for others.

2. Read the cloze passage in Question 1 with the students. Look at the words in the box and cooperate as a whole class "team" to work out where the words fit best to complete the sentence. Allow the students time to complete their own sentence using words from the box.

3. Direct the students to the craft activity at the bottom of the page. Read the words written inside each of the people and the words in the boxes. Have the students predict what the words in the tower will read when it is constructed.

4. Read the instructions for completing the craft task and demonstrate how the puzzle is to be put together as a model for the students.

5. Allow the students to color, cut and glue the pieces onto a separate sheet of paper.

Follow-Up Suggestions

Provide small-group developmental activities for the students to participate in where they are able to work cooperatively as a team. Suitable activities could include measuring tasks where the students are required to order capacities or weights by comparing different items, ball games where the students are required to share equipment, construction tasks where a set goal of building something "tall" or "long" has been given, or arts and crafts tasks where the students are required to share resources.

Sensitivity Issues

This activity is designed to illustrate how our attitude and behavior determine our ability to become part of a cohesive team. Positive self-esteem can be promoted through maintaining a safe, friendly atmosphere, in which students are required to follow the simple philosophy of caring for themselves and each other.

Activity Links

Answers

1. Work, together, friendly, happy (or happy, friendly)
2. Teacher check

We can all get along if we take care of ourselves and each other.

1. Use the words in the box to finish this sentence.

   Friends can _____ and play _____ when

   they are _____, caring and _____.

   | happy   together   friendly   work |

2. Cut out the people holding the blocks and glue them onto a separate sheet of paper to build a tower.

FOOD AND EXERCISE DIARY

Name

	Food				Exercise
	Breakfast	Lunch	Dinner	Snacks	Type/ Time spent
Monday —— date					
Tuesday —— date					
Wednesday —— date					
Thursday —— date					
Friday —— date					
Saturday —— date					
Sunday —— date					

Self-Esteem – Book 1

A HEALTHY LIFESTYLE

HEALTHY CHOICES

Indicators

- Completes a survey about his/her lifestyle.
- Tallies information from a survey.
- Interprets information from a table.

Teacher information

- Help students to complete the survey in Question 1 by reading each statement aloud and asking the students to indicate if they would be likely or unlikely to do each thing in a typical week in their lives.
- Once the surveys have been completed, ask the class to indicate their answers to each statement through a show of hands. With the students' help, teachers can tally the numbers on the board. The students can then copy this information into the table in Question 2.
- Have the students complete Question 3 independently. Discuss possible reasons for the majority answers in 3 (c); e.g., "Junk food is more tasty than fruit."

Additional activities

- Have pairs of students devise their own simple lifestyle surveys to try out on the class.
- Write a list of healthy class goals based on the results of the survey. Students can report on their success.

Answers

Answers will vary

A HEALTHY LIFESTYLE

Healthy Choices

1. How healthy is your lifestyle? Color *likely* or *unlikely* for each healthy choice.

Eating • I will eat more fruit than junk food.	LIKELY UNLIKELY
Exercising • I will exercise on at least three days.	LIKELY UNLIKELY
Sleeping • I will feel full of energy every morning.	LIKELY UNLIKELY
Relaxing • I will do something relaxing every day.	LIKELY UNLIKELY

2. How healthy are the lifestyles of your class members? Is it likely they will make healthy choices in the week ahead? Tally and total their answers. Include your answers.

	Likely to be healthy		Unlikely to be healthy	
	Tally	Total	Tally	Total
Eating				
Exercising				
Sleeping				
Relaxing				

3. (a) Color the area(s) in which most people were likely to be healthy.

eating	exercising	sleeping	relaxing

   (b) Color the area(s) in which most people were unlikely to be healthy.

eating	exercising	sleeping	relaxing

   (c) Discuss some reasons for these answers.

> **HEALTH CHALLENGE**
>
> *Write one healthy goal and try to stick to it for a week.*